EAT
NOURISH
FLOURISH

12 STEPS TO
HEALTHIER
FAMILY FOOD

CAREY DAVIS-MUNRO

EAT NOURISH FLOURISH

Thank you to Dr Robert Owen for your belief and guidance over the years

©2020 Carey Davis-Munro & Meze Publishing Ltd. All rights reserved

First edition printed in 2020 in the UK

ISBN: 978-1-910863-69-5

Author: Carey Davis-Munro

Edited by: Katie Fisher, Alice Horne & Phil Turner

Photography by: Paul Gregory

Designed by: Paul Cocker

Food & styling assistance: Lucy Fletcher

Contributors: Michael Johnson, Tara Rose, Paul Stimpson, Esme Taylor, Emma Toogood

Printed in Great Britain by Bell & Bain Ltd, Glasgow

Published by Meze Publishing Limited
Unit 1b, 2 Kelham Square
Kelham Riverside
Sheffield S3 8SD
Web: www.mezepublishing.co.uk
Telephone: 0114 275 7709
Email: info@mezepublishing.co.uk

CONTENTS

THE RECIPES

The recipes I am including here are flexitarian and family-friendly. That means that you choose the main ingredients according to the food preferences of whoever you're cooking for. I will usually start with a plant-based idea and give you options to flex it any way you wish; moving towards a plant-based diet is a journey, not a drastic change overnight, so being able to put yourself and your family somewhere on that scale is the first important step. Why do I think this is important? Because all current evidence and scientific data around long-term health and avoidance of lifestyle disease points to a plant-based diet.

The other reason I love this approach is it encourages you to move away from recipes, have a play with food and switch up ingredients. If you use the 'How to Stock Your Cupboards' section of this book (starting on page 165), you should have most of the things you need to hand. Not having to buy huge amounts of extra ingredients each time you try something new makes it much easier to experiment with your cooking, even on a weeknight.

However, I try not to be prescriptive in any of my recipes, so that your preferences and choices take centre stage. This is why I prefer to say "what I use" and "how I make it" instead of a list of set ingredients and a method. There are also elements of some recipes that you can easily mix and match with others; the raita, for example, goes brilliantly with both Aubergine Rogan Josh and Beetroot Tikki while the Potato Wedges, which I've shown with Baked Beans, can accompany any number of family dinners.

Because this book is aimed at you and your family, all of my recipes tend to serve four or five people, often with some leftovers to reheat for lunches (at school or home) the next day. You can scale the quantities up or down to suit your mealtimes, and make my suggestions work for you. Remember, making your way towards a healthier relationship with food isn't about denial; food should always be delicious, enjoyable to cook and to eat, with nutritional benefits that help you and your family stay well in the long term thanks to great meals every day.

INTRODUCTION

From spiralising veg to eating more plant-based meals, many of us have been inspired by the very talented people who are pioneering the way forward in healthy eating. We now take it for granted that it is only through eating well that we can ease rising obesity rates, combat chronic disease, and manage the extra pressure on our healthcare services. Equally, we know that establishing these habits early can set lifelong beneficial behaviours for our children.

Having worked in this area for over 25 years myself, I fully embrace this movement and delight in finding delicious new healthy foods and products on the market. I will support anything that raises awareness about eating well and that makes it easier to do so.

But making a commitment to a healthier path for yourself is a world away from bringing your family along with you. As a parent, you can't suddenly change your family's diet from meat-eating to vegan overnight or bin all those family favourites in one fell swoop as soon as you realise they don't provide the nutrients they should. You certainly won't be able to change your taste buds – or those of your family – just because you want to.

For positive change to be sustainable, gain the support of your loved ones, and have a long-lasting impact, it needs to be a process. You'll need to bring your family along with you, throughout the education, the understanding, the planning, the cooking, and – of course – the passion. And that's where I, as a food coach, come into it.

A food coach is not the same as a nutritionist; that isn't something I've ever aspired to be. I studied with the Institute of Optimal Nutrition, which was fascinating and inspired me to continuously and voraciously read and learn more about food and nutrition. But my work takes a different focus.

As a food coach, I feel privileged to work with amazing parents and carers who want to ensure they're giving their families the best basis for a long and healthy life. There are many complex psychological reasons as to why we don't invest the time, energy, and money in healthy eating, even though evidence shows that it is undoubtedly the single most important thing we can do for ourselves and our children. This is why I primarily focus on changing the relationship you have with food for the better. As part of this, I help tackle the practical side of changing long-term eating habits, support you and your family on the way, and generally help make eating well so much more accessible. Be that as it may, please keep in mind that the information provided in this book is intended to be general and, as such, isn't appropriate for those with exceptional dietary needs or conditions. If in doubt, it's always best to consult your doctor first.

Most importantly, I'm a mum with three teenagers. So, I understand the reality of dealing with fussy eaters, school stress, and the fact that maybe you don't have time to spiralise countless carrots every week!

Making any change is a matter of how you view your priorities and fully understanding why you're making that change, so I'm not going to put you through a programme and tell you exactly how to approach your transition to healthier eating. Instead, you will choose, find and create your own path that works for your unique family while I 'shine a light' on the route you're taking.

That said, in this book there is a basic framework you'll follow. I've called it a 12-step plan because there are 12 phases in this journey, but this is definitely not meant to be prescriptive. Approach each phase at your own pace; you can even change the order if you like. It could take a month, or it could take 12 weeks; it could even take 12 months. The important thing is that you're moving forward.

Chapter One sets you up on your journey with more detailed information about the plan and what to expect. To succeed in anything, you need to start with the right mindset, so Chapter Two begins your journey by digging deep into your own relationship with food and what has motivated you to change. Here, you'll set clear goals for your plan, which will act as a guiding light every week.

Chapter Three is where you start to put it all into practice. I'll take you step by step through every phase on your way to a healthier, happier family, right from getting your loved ones on board to stocking a healthy snack cupboard and learning how to 'go with the flow'.

And here's the yummy part: as you move through the 12 steps, you'll find some of my absolute favourite recipes. These have seen me through everything from chaotic family evenings to special occasions, and I hope you'll find something here that will become part of your trusted repertoire.

But this is so much more than a recipe book. It's about empowering you to make positive changes that will last and, ultimately, giving you and your family all the tools you need to live a long and healthy life. And that's where my 'toolbox' (see page 162) comes in: it's packed full of handy tips and tricks that can help you out at any stage. And since teenagers come with their own unique set of problems, you'll find some advice here specifically relating to these turbulent years, (see page 170) though of course feel free to skip this if it's not relevant to you!

Turn the page, and let's get started!

Carey

PRELUDE

As I write this nine weeks into the UK's Covid-19 lockdown, it would be remiss of me not to contextualise this book against the backdrop of what is happening in the wider world.

Since we went into lockdown there has been continual talk of 'getting back to normal'.

I don't want to go back to the way things were.

The way things were got us here. The way we treat our planet. The way we treat the other animals we share our planet with. The way we think about and treat our food. The way food and eating is incidental and dispensed with at speed in this 'more, quicker, harder, faster' world we live in. Where we can have everything, and invariably do at the click of a button. Where our priorities are skewed and we live life on a virtual treadmill.

Food has been a theme throughout this period, whether the focus is on empty supermarket shelves — partly due to people hoarding ingredients for themselves far beyond need — or the issue of constant snacking for those at home that we are seeing all over social media. There's also the food banks and soup kitchens that have simply not been able to provide anything near the amount of food needed for people suffering hardship at this time.

The Covid-19 pandemic will see more than a quarter of a billion people suffering from acute hunger by the end of the year according to new figures from the WFP (World Food Programme). When some of us may think we have had it hard in our privileged positions in the UK, there is no hint of a comparison to those living in conflict zones at this time.

Poor nutrition leaves children especially vulnerable and it is vital that commercial trade continues to flow, as humanitarian work depends on it. That throws up questions and problems in itself, however. Worldwide hoarding continues, countries are putting up trade barriers and the WFP's chief economist Arif Hussain says, "Just like in developed countries where governments are doing all they can to assist their people, we need to do the same for tens of millions of people." This is an impossible task to be faced with.

I have taken part in two Food Summits since lockdown, where panels of world-renowned doctors, scientists, nutrition experts and writers have discussed the roots of Covid-19 and the direct link to the way we produce food here in the UK and worldwide.

Although the outbreak was initially tied to a market in Wuhan, there is emerging evidence that suggests the virus began spreading in the community in October before being recognised as Covid-19. This brings us to examine the way animals are bred all over the world, but particularly in the wildlife trade. The immune systems of animals who are kept in awful conditions are weakened, and this results in a combination of species and pathogens leading to mutating viruses that can spread very easily from species to species.

Although the Covid-19 outbreak has led to more regulations because of public pressure around the wild animal trade, it is thought the restrictions are narrow and won't last long enough or go far enough.

Global food production also presents a huge challenge to wildlife. For example, the beef industry is responsible for at least 80% of rainforest destruction, illegal and otherwise, and the emergence of new pathogens tends to occur where humans are changing landscapes forever by farming intensively and building larger communities. In the process, we are destroying ecosystems, diminishing biodiversity, and exposing ourselves to new viruses. Meanwhile, we as a species are also developing a resistance to antibiotics. The World Health Organisation says that "antibiotic resistance is one of the biggest threats to global health, food security and development today. Antibiotic resistance occurs naturally but misuse of antibiotics in humans is accelerating the process."

You would think we had learned the most valuable lessons from the breakouts of SARS in Chinese wet markets linked to Civets in 2002, Australia's 1992 Hendra virus from the treatment of horses, camels implicated in the Middle East Respiratory Syndrome in 2012 and chimpanzees hunted for bushmeat linked to Ebola in 2014. But instead of these cases leading to urgent action and huge changes, we are now faced with Covid-19. Who knows when this may end, or what new viruses may follow. The five trillion agribusiness industry "is in a strategic alliance with influenza," argues evolutionary biologist Rob Wallace.

So I for one do not want to go back to what we had before. What we have right now includes:

People having time to cook in their kitchens from scratch.

Children baking and using ingredients they haven't experimented with before.

People questioning the origins of the food they are eating.

Families eating together again, allowing time for valuable discussion. Time I thought I would never have again with my older teens has been the biggest gift for me.

Using substitute foods because the usual wasn't available and in the process widening cooking repertoires, creating learning and growth.

A recognition and a change in priorities; we really see now that if we don't have our health, we have nothing.

A slow acknowledgment that our food is directly linked to our immunity and we have the power to strengthen this ourselves: to maintain a healthy and thriving gut as the control centre for everything else that goes on in our body and mind.

We need change.

We need to think about the way the world organises food production. We need to recognise that food is the cornerstone to future-proofing this precious planet for our children and generations to come. We need to recognise that food is the cornerstone of our own individual futures: our physical and mental health and wellbeing.

Our planet must be protected. To avoid future pandemics, unsanitary means of production have to end and we must dramatically reduce dairy and meat farming, eliminating factory farming altogether. As human beings, privileged to share our planet with such an amazing array of life, we must take responsibility for and stop the barbaric treatment of animals.

Food is a fundamental need for us all. We share this responsibility to make it a global priority. It is our worldwide common denominator. 'We are what we eat' has a much deeper and more poignant meaning right now.

As I create this book amidst a worldwide pandemic, it is clear for many of us that we still don't have the priorities right: the building blocks of a future for ourselves, our children and our planet. Health, wellbeing and every mouthful we take has to be the focus. Because if not now, then when?

Let's take the responsibility for exactly what is in each mouthful. Where does it come from? How is it farmed? What are the effects on our planet and the creatures we share it with? Of course, we should also be ensuring that our food is nutritionally as well as ethically sound.

What changes will you be making?

Because if a pandemic will not prompt you to do so, what will? I sincerely hope this book will be life changing if you follow the process within it, and that you will emerge on the other side with a newfound understanding of and passion for food and your own nourishment of mind, body and soul. Commit to making it work and there is no better gift you will ever give yourself, or others… or that I could give to you.

CHAPTER 1

MY
APPROACH

There are several fundamental principles that underpin the approach used in this book. Whether they help you keep a positive mindset or provide extra motivation along the way, they are all intended to help you on your journey towards healthier eating.

COUNT NUTRIENTS, NOT CALORIES

As soon as you mention calories, the focus is on denial. Counting calories is also not related to health: it's quite possible, for example, to consume relatively few calories and still be unhealthy. Instead, to help you build an ongoing healthier relationship with food, I want you to get excited about the benefits: what food can do for you, how incredible different combinations of ingredients can taste, and how it can make you feel. We can do this by noting the nutrient value: the properties of foods and their benefits.

THINK OF YOUR MOUTH AS THE GATEWAY

Your teeth are there for a number of reasons, but I like to think of them as a gateway! They are like a 'stop point' for you to evaluate what you are about to put into your body. Before you do so, take a moment to check yourself: read labels on your foods, understand what it is you are eating, and enjoy every second of this rewarding process.

LET FOOD BE YOUR PHARMACY

Proactively managing the health of my children has also meant not relying on the bottle of Calpol in the cupboard, finding alternatives to antibiotics (or at least trying everything else I possibly can before resorting to them), and managing everything from conjunctivitis to tonsillitis – even anxiety – by first looking at what we can do with diet. For example, we can build immunity via healthy gut function – which is now widely recognised as our second brain – by looking at natural and sometimes age-old, tried-and-tested remedies.

With diet, you don't get the 'silver bullet' effect you might from medication, but then again, medical 'cures' don't eliminate what caused the ailment in the first place. A fever, for instance – as long as it is not at a dangerous level – is only telling us that our bodies are fighting off an infection. In other words, it is simply letting us know what is happening in the body.

THE TRIANGLE OF HEALTH: A WORD ON STRESS

I base my philosophy around the premise that optimum health centres on three things: good nutrition, enough exercise, and enough sleep. There is, however, one other factor that has a significant effect on our health and it is not quite as easy to control: stress.

Firstly, it's worth being mindful of the theory that it is not the stress itself that does us damage, but our reaction to it. As parents, we are constantly faced with stressful challenges related to our children, and this doesn't get any easier as they grow up. There are certainly ways we can try to minimise the harm that stress wreaks on our mental and physical health, simply by acknowledging our reactions to events and situations. But I would also suggest that cumulative stress – often as a result of events that are not in our control – has the potential to cause long-term damage to our overall health. As I was diagnosed with stress-induced chronic fatigue a few years ago, this is certainly the case for me.

So while this book is written from the viewpoint of examining – and managing – the long-term benefits of good nutrition, I am not here to tell you that this has solved all my problems. I would be lying if I said that.

But what I will say is control what you can. While we can't always control external stressors, we can generally choose what we eat, make sure we exercise, and get ourselves into bed at a decent hour. Getting these three basic things right can only have a positive impact on our stress and how we handle it. If I wasn't living this way, I don't think I would still be here, and certainly not living life the way I do.

BE A PARENT

I took part in a very interesting online summit not so long ago which focused on, among other things, the new science emerging around plant-based diets and the consequent benefits for our long-term health. I tuned in to several keynote speakers, many of whom were trained doctors in one area of medicine or another. One interview stood out to me so much that I ran to get my children so that they could watch too. He was essentially talking about the mantra I've repeated to my children endlessly over the years: 'You can't have that; I love you too much.'

This particular doctor was asked the question of how to enforce a healthy diet for our children with all the push back we might get, the habits they might be used to, and in the context that they will be different from their friends. His answer: how do you do anything as parents and enforce something that you know is right for your children? He asked, would you let them have alcohol? Would you let them smoke? How quickly would you make sure that they stopped?

In short, he said "be parents." We spend our whole lives devoted to doing what is best for our children: helping them with school work, taking them wherever they want to go, supporting their teams from the sidelines, just about anything they need. Why, then, do we find it so hard to take important decisions on what they eat and put in their bodies when it is the single most important thing that we, as parents, can do for ourselves and for them?

His comparison to cigarettes and alcohol is not a scare tactic either. He truly believes – as I do – that we do every bit as much damage with a poor diet as with other forms of self-abuse. In an exposé on television called The Truth About Meat, one bacon sandwich and the potential damage this can cause us was compared to smoking four cigarettes. Yet how many of us would serve one up as a treat for our children on a weekend?

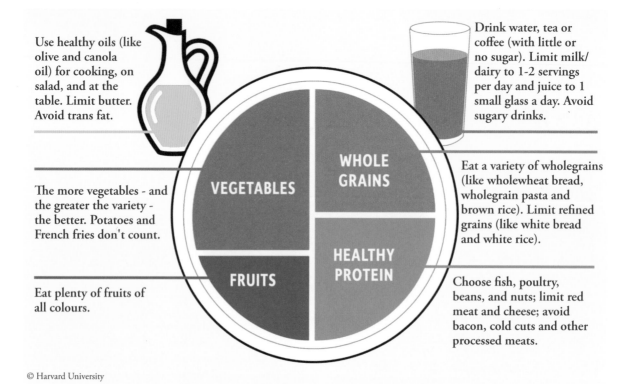

The more vegetables - and the greater the variety - the better. Potatoes and French fries don't count.

Use healthy oils (like olive and canola oil) for cooking, on salad, and at the table. Limit butter. Avoid trans fat.

Drink water, tea or coffee (with little or no sugar). Limit milk/dairy to 1-2 servings per day and juice to 1 small glass a day. Avoid sugary drinks.

Eat a variety of wholegrains (like wholewheat bread, wholegrain pasta and brown rice). Limit refined grains (like white bread and white rice).

Eat plenty of fruits of all colours.

Choose fish, poultry, beans, and nuts; limit red meat and cheese; avoid bacon, cold cuts and other processed meats.

VEGETABLES

WHOLE GRAINS

FRUITS

HEALTHY PROTEIN

© Harvard University

This is about re-framing what has long been acceptable in our minds, changing our habits and behaviours, and finding substitutes that will make the transition a pleasant one and sustain long-term change. I'm certain that no parent would allow their child to smoke four cigarettes for breakfast!

THE 80% RULE

This figure is significant for several reasons in this book. Firstly, the Japanese practice of hara hachi bu teaches us to eat until we are 80% full. Hara hachi bu is practised by the Okinawan people, who are renowned for living longer and being healthier than almost any other people on the planet.

Most of us simply eat and eat until we are full and then end up feeling quite bloated. So how can we know when we have eaten 80%? This is about re-setting the muscle memory of the stomach so we get less used to that 'full feeling' which means we've actually eaten more than we often need. It takes the stomach about 20 minutes to communicate to the brain that we are full, and by then it is too late. Instead, start by putting much less on your plate, perhaps 50 to 75% of your usual amount. Once you've eaten it, let your food go down and then see how you feel. You might need to adjust as necessary,

but eventually you will train that muscle memory so it knows when to stop!

Secondly, when you look at your plate (and your shopping list) it should resemble something like the diagram above: the Harvard Healthy Eating Plate. Aim for approximately 75 to 80% vegetables, wholegrains, and fruits, then add in your sources of protein, including beans and nuts.

Finally, 80% is about giving yourself a break. We start the job of being a parent with no experience and without necessarily having the skillset in place, and yet we all strive to be perfect as we want the very best for our children. Then, when we – inevitably – get things wrong, we are very quick to beat ourselves up.

Personally, I am done with beating myself up and I invite you to stop doing so as well. Acceptance is something I am learning later in life through yoga, along with humility in that I cannot be the best at everything and will make mistakes, not least in my parenting. This translates into every aspect of our lives, food included. So get yourself on the spectrum; I believe that if you are eating an optimum diet 80% of the time, then you are doing OK. Making your habits sustainable, achievable, and enjoyable is more important than killing yourself to do something perfectly. Perfection is not reality.

CREATING YOUR OWN HEALTHY FAMILY FOOD PLAN

WHAT TO EXPECT

"The mind is like an umbrella. It functions best when it is open." – Walter Gropius

Every family is unique – with different dietary needs, preferences, and challenges – which is why I haven't created a one-size-fits-all plan. Instead, this book uses a combination of mentoring and the powerful tried-and-tested GROW coaching model to help you make long-term, sustainable changes that are right for you and your family.

THE 12 STEPS

I've identified 12 steps, or phases, that I believe will give you all the tools you need to establish and maintain healthy eating for your family. They include everything from involving your family in the process to stocking a healthy snack cupboard. These steps, along with the 'toolbox', (see page 162) provide what I think of as the mentoring.

Unlike face-to-face mentoring – which can progress organically – in this book, I've had to suggest an order for the steps you might want to take. That said, they are designed to work just as well as a 'pick and mix' approach. You are in charge of your direction, and the pace and order with which you move through the steps and Toolbox should be influenced by your weekly goals. It is your personal journey, but use the book for guidance and resources, adapting and changing to suit you when necessary. You may even want to add some of your own steps, and that's brilliant.

THE GROW MODEL

Originally developed by Sir John Whitmore in the 1980s, the GROW model is a framework used for problem solving and goal setting. GROW stands for:

Goals
Reality
Options
Will

Each represents a stage of the process. At each stage, you'll answer questions to help raise your awareness about what is happening at present, set meaningful goals, and help you decide on realistic, achievable actions to get there.

Before you start making any changes, I'll guide you through these four stages to set you up with the best mindset for the journey. You'll also revisit these stages every week to check in on your progress and make new plans for the week ahead. We'll begin by establishing the following:

Your Goals: your main motivation or reason for starting this journey. This will help you identify an Ultimate Goal, which is where you want to be in three to four months' time. This has been proven to be roughly how long it takes to set habits that stick and are sustainable.

Your Reality: where you are now and exactly what is happening in terms of your healthy eating.

Your Options: a number of 'quick win' actions and Journey Goals (small, achievable and meaningful targets) for your first week.

Your Will: your motivation to do what you've set out to do, including identifying who you may need help from, and uncovering any foreseeable barriers.

Then, every week, you'll go through the same reflective process. This enables you to assess your achievements and wins from the week before, set new Journey Goals, establish exactly where you are in relation to that goal, and then put in your possible options for the week ahead.

GETTING STARTED

You may decide that you want to work through this book with someone else: perhaps a friend, colleague, partner, or relative. If you have older children, you could even go through this journey with them. Having a partner on this journey will help keep you accountable, so you aren't tempted to take shortcuts, procrastinate, or self-sabotage. It can also help to hear yourself discuss your thoughts out loud.

If you do so, take a moment to think who the best person for the job would be, and arrange a date and a time as soon as you can for your first session.

Then, you'll need:

- **A workbook of some sort to record the work you will be doing: somewhere to make notes as you move through the process**

- **A pen**

- **And, most importantly, an open mind**

Let's get started!

CHAPTER 2

YOUR
GOALS

GETTING CLARITY ON YOUR OBJECTIVES

When you start a journey, you need to know where you're going (your destination or, as I call it, your Ultimate Goal) and have worked out what steps (I call them Journey Goals) you need to take to get there. Your family's journey to healthy eating is no different, so it's important to spend a decent amount of time setting your Ultimate Goal now, and then, as you work through the phases, your Journey Goals.

SET YOURSELF UP FOR SUCCESS

Having a clear Ultimate Goal doesn't just give you a clear direction of travel; it also guides your attitude and mindset, which are two of the most important factors in helping you successfully reach your destination. With this in mind, this section will help you:

Work out where you want to be when you've completed your journey successfully

Crystallise your vision of what success will look like

Phrase your Ultimate Goal positively so that it remains at the forefront of your mind

Setting goals connects our subconscious to our conscious mind, so you may well find the process empowering and motivating in itself, and you may start to notice an immediate difference in your behaviour. Greater awareness alone can make a substantial difference to our habits in many areas, and especially so when it comes to food: we become mindful of what we're putting into our bodies and start to question and check ourselves, our desires and our actions.

In fact, many of my clients start making changes from the moment they book a session with me so that by the time we start, they have already mentally gone some way to committing to the change and starting the process.

Just by buying this book, I am sure you have raised your awareness to a new level and are far more conscious of the way you are eating. If so, you are already on the right trajectory to change your relationship with food!

TAKE YOUR TIME

No matter how keen you are to get started, do not rush this process. The longer you spend working on your mindset, the more meaningful your goal and your connection to it will be, which will give you the best possible chance to make sustainable changes. This section should take you at least an hour to complete.

That said, the tools are optional: only implement them if they add clarity to your process. Think of it a bit like a recipe, using ingredients you like but perhaps omitting or substituting some to suit your own tastes.

FIND YOUR 'WHY'

Your Ultimate and Journey Goals will reflect your 'why': your reasons for embarking upon this journey; the motivation behind buying this book in the first place; what drives and motivates you.

For me, the 'why' is my children. A year before I had my first child, the first of three, my body crashed. I'd hammered myself in competitive sports from an early age, but this went beyond just feeling a bit worn out: I felt permanently exhausted and beaten up. My digestion had all but seized up; I was permanently constipated with the pain and discomfort that entailed. I suffered from cluster headaches, sometimes for weeks at a time, I had pain in my joints – especially my wrists – and I had an ovarian cyst that required surgery.

A friend recommended working with a nutritionist, who suggested a hair analysis. I now know the scientific evidence for this is questionable, but at the time the results terrified me. Without meeting me or knowing my name, the report I received listed my symptoms accurately and suggested that, if I didn't take action, my health would only keep getting worse and lead to chronic conditions in later life. For me, there was no question: I needed to make severe changes in my diet, and they needed to be immediate.

By the time I was a mum, I was sure that the single most important thing that I could do for my children was to nourish them optimally, to use food functionally as medicine and teach them to understand why.

There's a very good chance that, like me, your ultimate 'why' is your children: it's natural to want to make sure your values underpin how you feed and educate them and approach their health.

YOUR PRIORITIES

To get started thinking about your 'why', it's useful to write down your top six to ten priorities – the areas of your life that are most important. For example, you might include:

Family

Children

Friends

Health

Exercise

Career

Personal growth

Religion/spirituality

Holidays

Work

Retirement

Me time

Community

You may, of course, have some of your own reasons that aren't mentioned here.

Once you've done this, it can be interesting to put these into a 'Wheel of Life' (originally created by Paul J. Meyer, founder of Success Motivation® Institute) with scores out of 10 or 100 to represent how important these areas are to you and how fulfilled you feel right now in each. This will help you start to get an idea of what you want to change, your priorities, what needs rebalancing, and where you want to place your focus,

which will give you clarity on your 'why' and make your goal more meaningful. Concentrating on your health brings everything else you want to achieve, to have, to be, into stark focus, since you can't do one without the other.

Here are some example wheels for you to populate or consider.

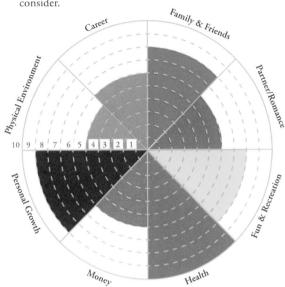

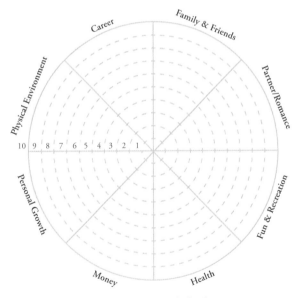

Changing your relationship with food means you are starting to future-proof your health. Instead of taking each day as it comes and seeing what it will bring, you are taking steps to proactively manage your wellbeing for the long term. This will also have an impact on your priority areas above and will start to bring everything into context: better health underpins everything.

SETTING YOUR GOALS

YOUR GOAL

Now you have more clarity about what's important to you, start thinking about your Ultimate Goal. It may help to ask yourself the following questions:

What do I want to get from going on this journey?

Why is this journey important to me?

What will it bring or give me?

What will it look like when everything's happening the way I want it to? Write down what you see in your mind: visualisation is powerful.

How will it affect my relationships? (It always does! Everything is linked to our relationships...)

How will it benefit those around me?

How will it feel when I've achieved this?

What would I say to a friend who has successfully managed this?

And what will I say to myself when I'm successful?

When do I want to be in this position by?

If you're finding this difficult or are still unsure about your Ultimate Goal, that's fine. Even just a general idea of where you're headed is a very good, useful start, and the next parts of this section will help you refine it. You'll also have a chance to fine tune your Ultimate Goal after we've looked at your reality, and you will come back to it at the beginning of every week in the 12-step plan.

FRAME YOUR GOAL POSITIVELY

Our minds respond better to positives than negatives so, when setting your goal, make sure you frame it positively. For example:

"I want to feel less stressed about feeding my family," might become: "I will feel calm and in control where food is concerned, knowing I'm nourishing my family."

"I want to stop my children eating so much rubbish!" might become, "I will teach my children the difference between healthy and unhealthy food by giving them the best I can."

Avoid words that focus on the issue or problem, such as:

"I want..." or "I need..." – these phrases affirm that you are lacking something

"I'll try..." – this affirms you will attempt to do something, not that you'll succeed

You should also avoid conditionals, such as "If I get this promotion" or "Maybe I could". Instead, you want definite statements. Choose words that focus on what you're going to achieve, such as:

"I will..."

"I have..."

"I shall..."

"When..."

"To" and "achieve" are powerful first words for a goal. For example:

To improve...

To enhance...

To support...

To promote...

To increase...

To raise...

To create...

To achieve…

What does your Ultimate Goal look like at the moment?

Write it here:

CHECK YOUR ULTIMATE GOAL

Now you have an idea of what your Ultimate Goal will look like, it's a good idea to check that it aligns with your reality. Ask yourself:

Does it reflect my values?

Does it capture my 'why'?

Is it SMART?

Specific: Is my goal well defined?

Measurable: How will I know when I've achieved my goal?

Achievable: Will I actually be able to attain my goal?

Realistic: Do I have the necessary resources, including time and money?

Time-bound: Is there a timeframe for my goal?

If you're stuck, you can find some examples of my clients' Ultimate Goals at the end of this section. Take inspiration from them to find something that resonates with you.

When you're satisfied with your Ultimate Goal, write it here.

My Ultimate Goal is:

KEEP IT REAL

Having your Ultimate Goal ever-present in your consciousness will dramatically increase your chances of reaching it. So, using anything you like – the computer, paper and pens, pencils, paints – create a piece of artwork that reminds you of it. Use your favourite colours, symbols, and other design elements to inspire you. It doesn't have to be complicated to be effective! Then, stick a copy on the fridge, use it as your screensaver, and keep a copy on a card in your purse or wallet.

You may well finetune your Ultimate Goal in the coming weeks, so a design that can be adapted is often best.

Here are some examples of goal artworks:

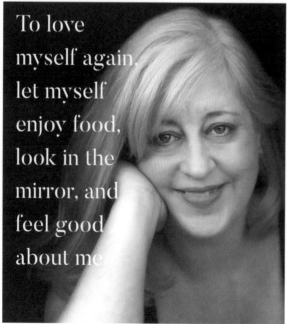

And, if you're still in need of inspiration, here are some examples of Ultimate Goals to stimulate your thinking, beginning with my own. Remember, there's no template: your goals are your own!

When I started this journey, my goal was to:

Manage my children's (and my own) health proactively to the best of my knowledge and ability.

Ensure they're optimally nourished and treated naturally where possible using healing foods.

Transfer my passion for food to my family and use it as a glue to bind us together.

Here are some goals chosen by people I've worked with:

"To upgrade the meals I already cook by using more nutrient-dense ingredients."

"To understand more about healing foods and to use them to support my family's health."

"To love myself again, let myself enjoy food, look in the mirror, and feel good about me."

"To create a rolling two-week menu of meals that I am happy and confident about cooking, knowing they are doing me good, adding something different as and when."

"To make food more of a family affair; to include everyone in the planning, cooking and clearing away."

"To use food to manage my skin, fatigue, and lethargy."

"To be able to share the same evening meal with my daughter at least twice a week."

"To feel comfortable and confident that the food I'm giving my daughters is the best possible in respect of nutrition and proactive health management."

"To eliminate all the junk my teenagers are eating and to replace it with healthy substitutes the whole family are happy with."

"To be inspired by food in a way I never have been before and try to communicate this to my children."

YOUR REALITY: WHAT'S REALLY HAPPENING?

Once you've identified what you want to achieve and have set your Ultimate Goal, the next step is to take a good look at what exactly is happening right now in your life in terms of food.

When I started my journey, I didn't have children – it was just my partner and me – so my reality was vastly different to what it is now, and I could make changes without resistance. But whatever stage you're at, being honest with yourself now will help you make better long-term changes.

At that time, I already had a powerful motivation: I knew I wanted to have children very soon and I was worried about what would happen if I didn't make the necessary changes. My body had to be ready!

Given a list of new foods to try, I accepted that I wouldn't embrace them all, but I knew I had to make the fundamental important changes: increasing the percentage of fruit and vegetables in my diet, the wholegrains, the good protein. I also needed to concentrate on good fats, to cut out the junk and – I decided – caffeine and alcohol. I learned that we are not just what we eat, but what our bodies can absorb. Be aware of this and all the interrelated systems in our bodies that have an impact on this. Learning to be reactive and responsive to our physical and mental self is all-important.

I realised I was the one preparing 99% of the food for myself and my partner. I was therefore doing the planning and shopping most of the time, which meant I had control over the changes I was going to make. However, we were eating out a lot and this was not helpful to our overall diet.

Food was also a highlight and a passion for us both, so it had to continue to be so. I could see that any changes would affect my partner, but only in a very positive way, and I needed to be able to articulate this in a way that got him on board.

Taking stock helped me plan my approach and what to focus on. The change would be driven by me, but I needed to have the support of my partner. As long as I could make mealtimes as delicious as they always had been, I wouldn't meet any resistance. We also needed to be more conscious of how often and where we were eating out. Frequent takeaways would be a thing of the past.

STARTING FROM WHERE YOU ARE

Start this process by asking yourself the questions below and answering as honestly as you can. Feel free to add in questions of your own. If this throws up thoughts, realities, or issues you hadn't expected, sit with them overnight, and write them down ready to discuss or come back to.

Again, it's important not to rush this: you'll only get the best out of this process if you spend enough time in each section, starting by examining your current relationship with food. 'Unpacking' your reality in this way shows you where you are now and how far you have to go.

You might even want to go through this process with your partner, a family member or friend. Examining what's happening – and the change you want to see – together in a safe environment can be a rewarding and supportive process.

Whatever you find, don't make judgments: you're moving forward! Everything we are doing here is future-focused.

Ask yourself the following and note down your responses:

What is happening right now in terms of food?

Describe what things look like, including but not limited to:

Who does the shopping, menu planning, cooking, preparing, and clearing away?

How often is food prepared from scratch?

Where does the food come from?

How important is food in our house? Where does it come on the list of our priorities?

What are my household members' food preferences?

Am I accommodating any allergies or different diets?

Describe mealtimes:

How confident and experienced a cook am I?

How often do members of my household eat together?

What makes up my diet right now? What proportion of my food is vegetables, fruit, meat, cheese etc.?

What is the result of all of this?

Who is affected?

How does this make me feel?

How is it affecting everyone involved?

How is it affecting my relationships?

What are our barriers to eating healthily?

Do I have any limiting beliefs regarding making changes to what I eat?

When did I start thinking about changing my family's relationship with food?

Why am I not currently preparing and eating healthy food as often as I would like?

How have outside influences (for example extended family, friends, school dinners, and travelling abroad) affected my family members' attitudes to food and eating habits?

Have I tried changing my family's relationship with food before?

If yes, what worked/what didn't work and why? What happened? Where was my motivation lacking?

If no, why am I starting this journey now?

What have I done already towards my goal?

If you knew there were, for example, ten things you needed to do to get to your goal, which would you do first? What is that action that will propel you forward the most?

At the end of this process, come back to your 'why' – your reasons for embarking on this journey now – and your underpinning values. These will realign your thinking from where you are now to your Ultimate Goal and ensure your motivation remains on track.

Do you have a better idea now of your reality, and some of the things that need to change in order to get you to your goal? Do you feel you know what this will look and feel like once you are there? Sometimes by establishing what we don't want, we become clearer on knowing exactly what we do want!

WHY DON'T WE PRIORITISE HEALTHY EATING?

Did you know that, while cookery and food are amongst the most popular genres on British TV, we don't put much – if any – of what we see into action? Despite cookery shows' popularity, studies show they neither inspire us to reproduce the meals we see prepared on screen in our own kitchens, nor instigate change in our eating behaviours.

Feeding our loved ones the best food possible is one of the most important things we can do for their health, longevity, and quality of life. So why, more than a decade after the benefits of healthy eating (and effects of unhealthy eating) came to the forefront of our national consciousness, do so many people still not see good food as a priority?

Even before the current Covid-19 crisis, the headlines were full of both NHS funding crises and diet-related illnesses, such as rising rates of obesity and Type 2 diabetes. During these very challenging times we have seen the death rates linked to obesity and diabetes; almost one in three people who have died in hospital after testing positive for Covid-19 had diabetes, according to the NHS research. While people with Type 1 diabetes were found to be three and a half times more at risk of dying from Covid-19, and those with Type 2 at twice the risk of those without, research shows that (up until 17th May 2020) 7,466 people who died from Covid-19 had Type 2 diabetes and only 365 people had Type 1 diabetes. "Higher blood glucose levels and obesity were linked to higher risk," according to the Nursing Times on 20th May 2020.

What we must take away from this is that Type 2 diabetes can be reversed and is led by lifestyle, while Type 1 is usually something you are born with and is genetic or environmental.

We have choices to make about our health and a lot is within our control.

By now we all surely know, at least on some level, the importance of proactively managing our own health. So why do we ignore the experts' advice, make so many excuses to ourselves and others, and push eating well to the bottom of the pile in our priorities?

We allow so much else in our lives to take up so much time – like most people nowadays, if I'm not careful, I can lose literally hours inside my mobile phone consuming a diet of digital rubbish – yet we don't focus on eating well and optimally nourishing ourselves. Why is this the case, when diet can make the difference between whether our children go to school or not, whether we can go to work or not, and whether we can exercise or socialise or not?

I have looked at many of the reasons people give for not prioritising healthy eating; here are some of the most popular and what you might do if they resonate with you. How many of these did you find when you looked at your reality?

The chief cause of failure and unhappiness is swapping what you want most, with what you want right now.

ZIG ZIGLAR

"I don't have the time."

How much time we feel we have is an important factor in many areas of our lives, especially how we all eat. Not having enough time is the top reason people give us for not prioritising their diet, and their family's.

If this is one of your reasons, ask yourself this: if you don't have time to prioritise what your family eats and your health, do you have time to be unwell? Does your family have time for you to be unwell? The truth is, eating well can create more time by giving us enhanced clarity and energy, making us less prone to sickness and extending our lifespan.

We make all our choices and decisions about how we spend our time based on what we see as our priorities. If good health, and the rewards it brings, are your priority, you'll find or make the time. Distinguish between your 'urgent' and 'important' as Stephen Covey advises and don't give away your time on the wrong things.

"It won't happen to me." (The Optimist)

While a 'glass half full' outlook on life is more enjoyable in general and, it can be argued, better for our mental health, did you know that pessimists live longer than optimists? That's because they're more prepared for all eventualities and take better care of themselves. Research shows that invariably, it takes illness or a real health scare for people to make a determined choice to change the way they eat.

I am no exception. In fact, on the contrary, I am a case in point. During my years of playing competitive sport, I didn't once pay any attention to what I was eating to support the immense amount of physical activity that I was doing. (I clearly remember loving Cuppa Soups and Arctic Rolls!) I know now that I was simply storing up no end of trouble for myself: I didn't listen to my body, until it was screaming.

If this is one of your reasons, a bit of realism might encourage you to take a longer, harder look at your lifestyle and make the necessary changes.

"I just don't like these 'healthy' foods / I like what I know and know what I like / Life's too short not to eat what you want."

This is understandable; everyone's taste buds are conditioned to like the sorts of foods they eat most regularly, foods with high fat and sugar content are known to be addictive and junk is designed to leave you craving more. But that's not to say that it's impossible to wean yourself away from sugar- and salt-laden foods, and fizzy drinks. It has to be done slowly, so that it's sustainable, and you need to find your replacements to make it achievable. But it can be done.

If this is one of your reasons, remember that you won't be the first person who has made the journey from preferences like yours to healthier replacements. When you decide to change how you eat for the better, a process of slow adaptation will follow as you wean yourself from one set of foods, tastes, and flavours to another much healthier set. If you persevere, you'll be amazed, not just at how much more enjoyable new tastes and flavours can become, but also how unappetising your old diet will seem in comparison!

"It's too hard."

This may contain some truth: it is indeed harder to plan, prepare, and cook meals from scratch. But again, it's harder still to be ill…

If this is one of your reasons, focus on how changing your diet will energise you, revive you and enable you to make the changes sustainable. This is about turning new practices into habits that become part of your lifestyle and making the process as easy as possible. The rewards are huge and the food becomes so much more delicious, enjoyable and rewarding! When you start to see and feel the difference it makes, you won't want to go back.

"If I'm going to get ill, I'm going to get ill – there's not much I can do about it."

If this is one of your reasons, well actually, yes there is. A devil-may-care attitude may well increase your risk of getting ill later in life, if not sooner. Fate will not have played a part in this; your own attitude will.

"All the conflicting claims about what's healthy are too confusing; I'll stick to what I know."

There is a lot of conflicting information out there, especially on the internet. However, while the science on food and its relationship to health can be contradictory and is continually changing, a general understanding has now emerged.

When I was planning this book and working on the research, my good friend and mentor Dr Robert Owen asked me how I was going to approach the fact that the overwhelming evidence base for both healthier eating and combatting disease supported a move towards a plant-based diet. My answer, to him and to you, is that we have to be honest about this.

From what information we have, from the science-based evidence and from our own experience, eating fewer animal products and processed foods is more beneficial in protecting us from disease and promoting longevity. In other words, healthier than the alternatives.

The debate about the healthy level of animal products in our diet is still raging; it's a very emotive and divisive subject and provokes passion on both sides. But remember: reducing the level of animal products we consume doesn't just affect human health and animal welfare. It's also significantly better for the environment because livestock rearing is generally far more resource intensive, in terms of land and water use among other factors, than growing crops.

If this is one of your reasons, read around these issues widely, as Dr Owen and I have done, and draw your own conclusions. Most of all, trust your common sense!

If you're not vegan or vegetarian, trial a decrease in the amount of animal-based foods in your diet and increase the amount of fruit, vegetables, beans, pulses, seeds, and nuts to make up the largest proportion of what you eat. The chances are, you'll soon see and feel the benefits.

The Vegan Society website is a good place to start your own research.

"It's in my genes – I can't change that."

We can, of course, carry predispositions to certain illnesses in our genes; my own three children have inherited a gene for a heart condition. However, I know that if they're fit and healthy, and if they exercise well throughout life and have an exemplary diet, this may never manifest beyond them simply carrying the gene. Their father is a good example: while he has been recommended statins for the condition, he has until recently preferred to continue to swim several times per week and follow an excellent diet.

If this is one of your reasons: remember, it's possible to carry a gene and to manage it carefully and well. Proactively managing our health dramatically decreases the risks of complications arising from genetic conditions.

"My family aren't onside and I don't want to upset them."

If this is one of your reasons: your loved one(s) will be onside pretty quickly when you communicate clearly your reasons for deciding to make changes (your 'why') and if the food you're all eating, far from being a hardship or representing denial, is delicious and nutritious.

Start with small changes and focus on adapting the meals and foods you all love to simply make them better. Don't draw attention to what you're doing, and remember baby steps are best when dealing with buy-in and resistance… I guarantee your loved one(s) will soon be on board. Step 4 is devoted entirely to helping you do this.

"I go to the gym regularly/run and burn off loads of calories, so I can eat what I like."

If this is one of your reasons: you simply can't outrun your fork! While exercise should form part of your healthy regime, it has recently been proven that, when it comes to managing our health, prevention of disease and indeed building our immunity, the single biggest contribution comes from the foods we're eating and the diet we're choosing. Exercise does not counteract or balance your three pints down the pub or your choice of fish and chips or pizza. Your body is not a bank account you can withdraw from and top up in this way.

"My job doesn't allow me to be home much and I eat out at lots of social occasions."

Again, this is about making the right choices when you have the opportunity to do so.

If this is one of your reasons, focus on getting in your fruit and veg, not to mention pulses, before you arrive at the social dinners and events so you won't fill up on the unhealthy offerings when you get there. There are some great food outlets now that will facilitate healthy eating on the go. It's about making this a priority in your busy day.

"If the children are hungry I need to have quick snacks around: I'd rather they have something not so good than nothing at all and go hungry."

If this is one of your reasons: the truth is, you'd be better off giving them nothing at all, rather than sugar-loaded snacks, crisps, drinks, and biscuits. Simply cut them out, take them off your shopping list, and replace them with healthier homemade or bought alternatives such as dried fruits and plain nuts. You don't have to have rubbish around the house so you can just give them 'anything'.

However many of these reasons you give to justify the fact that your family isn't eating healthily, ask yourself this: if you absolutely understood that your life, and your loved ones' health, depended on it, would you continue to make these excuses?

We can build ourselves a whole wall of obstacles and ideas that make providing healthy food difficult, or we can knock out the self-defeating bricks that make up that wall by using positive affirmations and asking ourselves questions that challenge our thinking.

For example:

What if I did have time?

What would that give me?

What would I do?

What if I did get seriously ill?

What changes would I make then?

How would I do that?

What if I did prioritise my diet and health?

What would I do then?

How would that change my life?

What if I realised things weren't so hard?

What if I found much easier ways to do things?

What if I found a healthier routine that fitted with my commitments?

What if I looked at some of the evidence that confuses me and made a choice to trust just a couple of experts I know, and like?

What changes would I make?

How would that make me feel?

Change your negatives into positives and take down your wall of obstacles completely.

Now that you've delved deeply into your own reality, and have full awareness and understanding of the dynamics of what's happening, the obstacles you may face, the excuses you may have made to yourself, the interactions that are impacting the situation, and how it's impacting your life and people in it, you're nearly ready to review your actions in the light of what you have learned.

Go back to your goals and sit with them for a couple of hours. Do they still reflect your 'why' and where you would like to get to? If so, then great. If not, then go back and tweak them to ensure they absolutely reflect where you want to be at the end of this process. Then put the latest version on your phone, computer, and fridge: anywhere you will be guaranteed to see it regularly and it will be part of your conscious day.

YOUR REALITY: EXPLORING YOUR RELATIONSHIP WITH FOOD

My work as a food coach is future-focused – as is all coaching – and that is what I absolutely love about it. We use our experiences of the past only to help us take steps into the future, and while I could never say we disregard feelings, in the coaching context, they are helpful purely in terms of how we will use them to move forwards.

With this in mind, you may find it productive to take a look at your own relationship with food up until now. You may not be very conscious of it, but through various stages of your life, your habits, influences, restrictions, and reactions will have changed for different reasons. As part of your journey to healthier living, understanding these factors can really improve your chances of sustainable success. Not only can this be fascinating, but it can be useful in helping define your 'why'. I went through this process when I began, and I was surprised at what I found. Perhaps you will be too.

WHAT IS A 'RELATIONSHIP WITH FOOD' ANYWAY?

We all have a relationship with food, whether we have seen it that way in the past or not. It is more than likely that this relationship is part of your subconscious. Our subconscious relationship with food not only instigates our reactions, but the habits we have built up and our feelings and associations around certain foods. Until you really start looking, you may not realise how this has affected how you eat the way you do today.

Sometimes, we can have one experience that guides our reactions and actions throughout our lives. When I was at primary school, for example, I was forced to eat processed mushy peas. The very thought of them now initiates a gag reflex in my throat and I have never touched them since. In fact, I would imagine that many of our negative reactions to certain foods stem from early school experiences.

Luckily, I have many positive associations from my childhood, too, and these have had a much more beneficial impact on the way I feel about eating and my food over the years. It has also determined the way I present it to my children.

LOOKING BACK

As with everything in this book, this reflection process is not prescriptive, but it may add context to your onward journey so I invite you to take what you will from this. The best way of doing this is to set aside some time with a friend, your partner on this journey, or similar.

Take it in turns to ask each other the following questions; you don't need to answer all of them. You can swap over either after each question, or after a set of questions. For this exercise, I am not going to suggest you write down your answers unless you want to. I feel this works far better as an organic conversation using the questions below simply to get you started.

Do you recall some of your first memories of food? How old were you? What was happening?

Were they positive? What do the memories evoke for you?

Who are the people involved in your first memories?

Can you remember what you ate at school? What feeling does this evoke for you?

What does the word 'diet' mean to you? Has it had any relevance to you over the years?

What was your favourite food as a child? Where did you have this, and who made it for you?

How have your eating habits changed and evolved over the years?

Would you eat the same foods you ate as a child or adolescent?

Have your finances had any bearing on what you have chosen to eat in the past?

What other influences have guided you to eat the way you do now?

WILL

In order to get your mindset right, understand your 'why', and ensure your motivation is as strong as it can be, we need to check in on your will. This is the final part of the GROW coaching model which we will look at in depth next chapter.

Each week, you'll set yourself your weekly Journey Goals, decide on your possible actions, and note specifically when and how you will do them. At this point, you will need to ask yourself where your 'will' is in terms of getting the actions completed: is your motivation as high as it can possibly be?

Ask yourself where your commitment sits on a scale of one to ten (where one is not motivated at all and ten is as motivated as you can get).

If your answer is below ten, ask yourself why your commitment is not at ten already? What you would need to do to get it there. Have you changed your 'why'? Is it still as powerful?

Then ask yourself whether there is anyone you may need help from to get those actions ticked off for the week in question. Is there anything you need to do to ensure they are completed? Any support you need to get in place?

This part of coaching is all about foreseeing your obstacles before you get going, understanding your commitment and acknowledging your motivation. Once you have this in place, you are well on your way.

CHAPTER 3

12
STEPS
TO
SUCCESS

12 STEPS TO HEALTHY EATING; FRAMED BY THE GROW MODEL

The 12 steps shown in this chapter and the GROW model outlined in Chapter Two form the framework for your journey towards healthy eating. Interspersed throughout this chapter, you'll also find a selection of recipe ideas that I hope will inspire you on your way.

These are all topics that I advise you to cover in your 12-step programme and are a vital part of reaching your goal. I've also put them in an order that I think gives you the best chance of success. It may be however, that you choose to cover them in a different order and set your own priorities; some of them might even happen concurrently as there is a lot to get organised initially. For example, for your family, it may be a priority to sort out the snacks you are eating first of all and get your substitutions in place. That said, it makes sense that setting yourself and your environment up for success should happen towards the beginning of your journey.

The whole programme is based on choice and empowerment, and you should see the following as a set of suggestions rather than instructions. Making any change is a matter of how you view your priorities, so I don't want to be prescriptive in how you approach yours. You dictate the pace, the actions and how and when you implement them.

As mentioned in Chapter Two, the GROW process runs through each week as a connecting thread. It encourages you to look at the previous week's wins, set new Journey Goals and decide on your options and actions. You may decide to build your goals around each of these 12 topics, but there is no need to be strict about this: allow for other topics to crop up so you can deal with them accordingly.

USING THE GROW MODEL

Come back to this section every week to check in on your progress and plan ahead.

WEEKLY GOAL SETTING

Spend 8 minutes minimum in this area.

This is where you will write your Journey Goal for each week throughout your journey, and maybe even beyond. Once you start setting goals, you won't stop: you will see how they affect your motivation and drive you to succeed and move forward in all areas of your life.

After the first week, ask yourself what two to three wins or 'learns' you experienced the week before. What were your biggest achievements? What were you most happy about?

Write your wins down clearly so you can refer back to them at a later stage. You may want to do this on a separate 'My Wins' page.

Each week, follow the original guidance used for your Ultimate Goal, in order to create your weekly goal. Ensure it is succinct, specific, and achievable.

Asking yourself the same questions we looked at for setting your Ultimate Goal – either by yourself or working with your chosen partner – check in on what this week's Journey Goal will bring you, what it will look like when everything is happening as it should, who it will affect, and perhaps what will happen if you don't do it. Play around with asking these questions in a different way and challenge your own limiting beliefs when you see them pop up. Ask new questions and note your reaction. It is OK to take yourself to some uncomfortable places; this is about getting your mindset right before you start.

Imagine what others may say to you about what you are doing. First, think about people you know: your grandmother, your favourite teacher at school. Then consider well-known figures who may cast a different perspective on what you are doing, perhaps Oprah Winfrey, Emmeline Pankhurst, Steve Jobs or Richard Branson.

Ask yourself who will be affected by this goal. What will it bring? How is it aligned to your core values?

As mentioned above, your Journey Goal may not directly relate to the step you are following, but it can run alongside it. Or you may like to follow the module and then build a goal around it. Remember, this process is about what works for you and what is important in your home. It's about your timings and your priorities, so make the goal as meaningful as you can and then sit with it while you go through the question process. It is vital to get yourself on board psychologically.

Once you have set your weekly Journey Goal, you will have your 'why' for the week, which connects to your Ultimate Goal and drives the impetus to make changes. This is all about raising your awareness and continuous learning. It will also connect your mind to your destination, which will start your new relationship with food.

REALITY WEEK BY WEEK

Spend 8 minutes minimum in this area.

As with your weekly Journey Goals, it is important to really understand where you are before you start each week. You can't just input a destination into your sat nav! You have to know where you are starting from and have your reference points planted firmly in your mind.

Again, look back on the original process and the questioning you went through with the Ultimate Goal to really get to grips with where you are on each new Journey Goal. Then ask yourself the following questions:

What have you done so far?

What is happening right now?

When have you done something like this before?

If you knew there were, for example, ten things you needed to do to get this done, which would you do first?

What would you tell your best friend if they were about to do this?

If you are going through this process with someone else, you can really start to challenge your thinking and delve deeper together. The learning and raising awareness is valuable.

It's important not to rush here. This is the 'anything is possible' option phase, so it's the time to really open your mind to new possibilities and ways of doing things, answers you may not have thought of before and valuable new learning. Sometimes even just understanding our reactions to feelings and acknowledging our automatic responses can be as valuable as achieving the goal itself. Embrace the discomfort: this is growth!

OPTIONS WEEK BY WEEK

Spend 8 minutes minimum in this area.

Your weekly options are all-important as they distil down all the thinking and reflection you've just done into a few actions that you want to take forward.

After thoroughly exploring your reality each week, you will be open to a whole world of options: all the things you could possibly do in an ideal world to reach your goal. For example, if your Ultimate Goal is to ensure that you are cooking and eating in the best possible way, your options might include starting to plan some healthier recipes, labelling your ingredients, or organising your kitchen differently. At this point, there should be no boundaries, no obstacles, no barriers, and certainly no limiting beliefs. You might even go as far as buying new cookware or a new oven!

Get all your options down on paper. It'll take 8 minutes at the very least to really generate enough ideas. Just when you think you have exhausted your well of ideas, go back again and ask yourself one more time: 'What else?' This is very often where the real gems come out.

I love options: they are the 'can do' part of coaching. They're about endless possibilities, moving forward and developing, learning, changing, challenging yourself. I often think of this as my fridge, full of the most delicious and nourishing 'forward foods' – foods that contribute towards good health rather than detract from it – that will do me good. Every day I go to my fridge of options and decide what combinations I will use to optimally nourish myself and my family.

ACTIONS WEEK BY WEEK

When you have your options set out and written down, you will be in a position to choose the one that for you is the priority. The one that shouts at you as being the thing you know you must do and that will propel you towards your goal. The one that will give you the most headway.

Then pick two or three others. Pick ones that feel similarly important. You may pick more or fewer options depending on how challenging and time consuming these actions are and the week you have ahead, but make sure you choose enough actions to take you forward, though not so many that you are overwhelmed.

Decide on when you will do each action and make it extremely specific: choose the day and the time and be as strict with yourself as you can. Alternatively, ask your coaching partner to check in on you here. It might also help to write them out as your clear weekly actions with the dates beside them. Make yourself accountable to yourself, and others if possible.

WILL WEEK BY WEEK

The final part of the process is to check in on your will to complete the actions you have decided on. As for your Journey Goal, if you have connected to your 'why' and have spent enough time on your goals and reality, you will already have the right mindset. But it is still useful to go through the following exercise.

Visualise a spectrum of positivity and motivation. Where do you sit on this spectrum at this point? Write it down as a number from one to ten.

If you are at less than a seven, ask yourself what you can do to get that number a little higher. What would it take? Who might you need help from? (It's really important to be able to recognise that we need and want help sometimes and it's a huge strength to be able to ask for it. It may be that you need to add an extra conversation into your actions to ensure it happens!)

Lastly, before you get started with your next step, ask yourself what learning you have taken away from the process you have just completed (with or without your coaching partner).

Write this learning down.

Another way of saying this would be to ask yourself: 'what am I left with' and 'where is my thinking at now'.

STEP

1

SET YOURSELF UP FOR SUCCESS BY ELIMINATING THE OBSTACLES

I've put this first because it is about preparation, and it is probably the single most important thing in getting going. If you do this thoroughly, you will remove so many of the obstacles to success, which – in my experience – is far easier than navigating round them! Eliminating obstacles is the difference between 'win' and 'lose'.

For this reason, you'll find more guidance and information in this step than in any other. But don't let that overwhelm you: everything that you are doing should be stretching you, not sending you into panic mode. Remember, I do not expect anyone to make all these changes from one day to the next: treat this as a guide. It's for you to decide which are the priority areas to address.

A. TAKE WILLPOWER OUT OF THE EQUATION

Set up your environment for success so that it works for you, and turn your kitchen into a haven. The principle is very simple: if you only have foods in your house and kitchen that are nutrient-dense, nurturing and 'forward' then you cannot go wrong. Here you'll be introduced to one of the most positive habits that I want you to get out of this programme. It will last you a lifetime and set you on a route to understanding exactly what every mouthful you put in your body is made of and in time, how it benefits you: checking all ingredient labels (see the Toolbox on page 162).

Get yourself a large, strong bin bag.

Go through your fridge, your kitchen cupboards, drawers and any other storage space and, for every item, find the ingredients and nutrition labels.

Look for any added sugars in any form on labels. Be aware that sugar can masquerade under many other names, such as corn syrup, fructose, glucose, sucrose, agave nectar, molasses, caramel, syrups, and maltodextrin. We call these 'free sugars' and our bodies simply don't need them. Beware: they will be in products you may not expect like cereals or cereal bars, which are often seen as healthy. Also check for yeast on labels. It is added freely into a whole host of products but can be disruptive to our gut health. I guarantee that you'll be surprised by what you find!

Then, ask yourself whether you want to let those foods past the gateway of your teeth. Will they help you achieve your goal or detract from it?

Anything that you've answered 'no' to – anything that is junk, sugar-loaded, artificial and preservative-loaded – put into the bin bag.*

You may want to leave some condiments while you get your substitutes in place, but generally, this is a move away from pre-prepared, long-life products, so this is the stuff you are trying to eliminate from your home. This should be quite a cathartic experience as you prepare to treat yourself and your family better!

At this point, it can also be helpful to consider what you are cooking with. If you use aluminium non-stick pans and coated utensils, they are doing you no good whatsoever: put them in your bin bag, too, and replace them with stainless steel or ceramic pans and a steamer. I don't mean an electric steamer but a good stainless steel pan with a couple of steamer pans that sit inside it; believe me this will one of your best friends. See the Toolbox on page 162 for more information on what to cook with.

*It's worth mentioning here that it's up to you what you do with the foods you have cleared out to create your haven. This may seem wasteful, but as with quitting smoking, if you only 'cut down', you are still telling yourself that it is OK. Of course, we must do all we can to minimise food waste, and you may want to donate them to a food bank. But I cannot, with a clear conscience, recommend keeping junk to anyone. It has no nutrient value and is really not the food and nourishment our bodies need.

B. ELIMINATE, UPGRADE, ADD IN

After you have removed everything from your home that contains empty calories or unhelpful, 'backward' nutrition – biscuits, crisps, sweets, white bread, white flour, doughnuts, croissants, white pasta, sugar-laden condiments, and ready-made packet foods – you are ready to make your first shopping list and start re-stocking your cupboards and fridge. This is a case of eliminating, upgrading, and adding in. You might find it helpful to refer to the How to Stock Your Cupboards section (see page 165), which provides more detail on addressing each area of your diet.

Eliminate. Go through your usual shopping list and take out anything that you may have just spent time eliminating from your kitchen: junk, snacks, empty-calorie (often white) foods, and any other foods that you may have considered 'treats' but that you know are not going to contribute to optimum nourishment.

Upgrade. Next look at 'upgrading' some of the other regular things you have on your list. By this, I mean take a look at some of the staples you buy every week and see if you can find ways of buying the same thing, but with a stronger nutritional profile: bread, pasta, rice, milks, juices etc. Use the How to Stock Your Cupboards section for healthier swaps.

Add in. Here is the fun part: trying new things! But not all at once. Again, using the How to Stock Your Cupboards section, pick one or two things each week that you would like to have a go at including in your shopping list. This might be something as simple as a new vegetable, a new type of grain, various types of beans and pulses, or an alternative fruit. You might also want to try new spices, herbs, rubs: the exciting things that are going to make the food you are eating absolutely delicious. Take some time standing at the spice counter,

understanding what they all are and how you might use them. Perhaps even visit a food market where they mix spices in front of you.

Now look at what your new shopping list is made up of. At least half of it should be fresh vegetables and fruit, forming the majority of your shop, with the other half split between healthy protein and good wholegrains. (Note: potatoes don't count because of their negative effect on blood sugar but sweet potatoes do!)

The same theory should translate into a plateful of food: each meal time should be at least 50% vegetables and fruit. Bear in mind that, in the UK, it is now recommended that we consume ten portions of fresh veg and fruit a day, not the five that we've become so familiar with over the years. This may seem a lot to begin with, but once you start adding vegetables and pulses into foods wherever you can, you will find that it becomes a habit. In fact, you'll probably get through these foods very quickly and you will need to start planning for mid-week 'top-up' shops.

It can be very helpful to go through the same 'wheel of life' exercise that you did when setting your goals (see page 25), but this time based on your shopping list or plate. Include all the food areas and groups you currently use and give each a mark out of ten for where you believe you are on optimising the nourishment of these foods. For example, snacks: on a scale of one to ten, where does your snacking sit right now? Make adjustments in the areas of most concern.

If you struggle with 'adding in' at first, you may need to take it more slowly. Start by adding in more of what you already like. This will gradually get your stomach and your taste buds used to having more of what you 'know and like' that is already healthy. Then introduce something new, perhaps something that you haven't tried before.

For example, try standing at the fresh fruit and vegetable counters: see which colours and textures appeal to you and aim for something different each week if possible. When you have exhausted the range, begin to rotate. Bit by bit, you will widen your range of ingredients and start to change your and your family's taste buds. They will gradually regain the ability to define more subtle tastes and flavours that will have been numbed by the sugary foods and flavour enhancers. Your gut will start to communicate with your brain in the way it is supposed to.

QUICK WINS AND EASY SWAPS

Bake sweet potatoes instead of regular potatoes for tasty and nutritious jackets.

For any pasta-based dish, use spelt wholegrain pasta and squeeze in six veggies, such as garlic, onion, peppers, mushrooms, spinach, broccoli, and cherry tomatoes.

Swap white rice to Camargue, mixed wild rice, brown rice, or a combination with mixed-grain quinoa.

Ditch regular chips for healthier wedges and roasted vegetables, such as sweet potato, cauliflower, and beetroot.

EVERYDAY PANCAKE MIX

My pancake mix has changed and evolved over the years. Now that I am 100% plant-based, I simply eliminate the eggs and thicken the milks using organic apple cider vinegar. I also use plant-based butter. It is so simple and gets great results each time. I also play around with the flours; purple cornflour works a treat but I mix this with spelt which is more reliable to cook with, and will often add a bit of ground almond too.

Preparation time: 5 minutes | Cooking time: approx. 20 minutes | Serves: 4 (2 pancakes each)

WHAT I USE

420g organic spelt or buckwheat flour
2 teaspoons baking powder
Pinch of rock salt
700ml milk of your choice (I use a mix of organic soya, almond and oat milk)
1 tablespoon apple cider vinegar (use one with the mother included)
50g butter or oil of your choice (plus a little extra for the pan)

HOW I MAKE IT

Put the flour, baking powder and salt in a large mixing bowl and stir with a whisk to ensure there are no lumps. Make a well in the centre .

Measure the milks into a jug then add the apple cider vinegar and stir it through. You will see the liquid thicken slightly. Slowly, add the milk bit by bit to the flour, gradually bringing in all the flour round the edges. Continue adding the liquid until the mixture turns from a stiff dough consistency to a fluid, smooth consistency.

It's down to you how runny you like the batter; if you like thicker pancakes and a more American style, add less liquid. Finally, melt the butter, then pour it into the pancake mix, or add the oil, and stir well.

Meanwhile, heat a frying pan on a medium heat. I use a ceramic pan for pancakes. The key to great pancakes is a super hot pan so I turn on the heat when I'm making the batter. Grease the pan with a little oil or butter, then add a ladle of pancake mixture to the pan, swirl it round to get an even thickness and let it cook. When you see it bubble on top, the pancake is ready to turn over. I prefer to flip with a fish slice, since I find this easier and it makes less mess! When flipped, cook the pancake for a further minute until it is lightly browned on both sides. Repeat.

Serve the pancakes immediately. You can use this recipe with both sweet and savoury toppings. We do this much like homemade pizza night: lay out all the toppings, bring the pancakes over and let everyone do the rest!

GRANOLA

Making your own granola is so simple, and so much fresher and more delicious than buying it! This way you can throw all the things that you like in there and personalise it. I use the ingredients below according to preference, and quantities to suit my storage containers.

Preparation time: 5 minutes | Cooking time: 20-30 minutes | Serves: depends on your quantities and ratios

WHAT I USE

Oats

Coconut oil

Coconut sugar

Coconut chips

Linseeds

Chia seeds

Mixed seeds (such as sunflower, pumpkin and sesame)

Banana chips

Goji berries

Other mixed dried fruit

Mixed nuts

HOW I MAKE IT

Preheat the oven to 180°c. Put three tablespoons of coconut oil onto a large baking tray and place it into the oven. Take out after only a minute or so when the oil has melted.

Place four large handfuls of oats into the oil and mix really well, ensuring it is all covered. I do this using the back of a spoon to really push the oats into the mixture. If you'd like any sweetener, I suggest minimal amounts of coconut sugar sprinkled over the oats at this stage.

Place the tray back in the oven for about 20 minutes, taking it out every now and then to stir the oats and ensure they are all toasting evenly. Take out when they are done to your preference and have that lovely toasty aroma, then leave to cool.

Add in all the extras, using more or less depending on your preferences. Mix well and store the granola in airtight containers.

Delicious with fresh berries, coconut yoghurt and a large dollop of homemade chocolate nut butter (see recipe on page 68).

BREAKFAST SMOOTHIE

This is everything you need for a healthy gut, mind and energy level all day, plus a minimum of three portions of fruit and veg before you walk out the door. For over 18 years, I have made myself (and my children when they came along) a smoothie for breakfast. Although I tend to throw in a huge variety of different fruits depending on what I have in the house, this is my base.

Preparation time: 5 minutes | Serves: 4

WHAT I USE

Depending on the size of your blender, amounts are going to vary but in my NutriBullet (I use two jugs to make four large smoothies) I use the following:

2 bananas, peeled

2 large handfuls of spinach

4 broccoli florets

4 large strawberries

3 tablespoons blueberries

1 tablespoon raspberries

1 tablespoon goji berries

2 teaspoons chia seeds

1 tablespoon flax seeds ,ground or whole (it blends in the NutriBullet)

1 teaspoon bee pollen

2 brazil nuts

3 almonds

2 large tablespoons yoghurt of your choice (I use nut yoghurt as I prefer to avoid dairy, but kefir would be a great way to get your fermented foods in)

Almond milk or coconut water and pressed juice

Optional

½ an avocado (this makes the smoothie really creamy if you prefer not to add any yoghurt)

3cm fresh turmeric (I often add this which is fruity and distinctive)

HOW I MAKE IT

Simply place all the ingredients into your blender or split into two jugs as I do. Either fill your blender with almond milk or with three quarters coconut water and one quarter pressed juice of your choice.

Once the liquid has been added, blend until absolutely smooth. Serve and drink immediately.

Tip: Frozen fruit is JUST as good as fresh in smoothies!

HEALTHY MILLIONAIRES

Known as 'Chocolate Yummy' in our house, this is my 100% plant-based alternative to chocolate-covered digestive biscuits and Millionaire's Shortbread. I'm aware this is a long list of ingredients, but if you don't have everything for the base, it can be made just with oats and nuts. The other ingredients add extra nutrient value; carob is naturally sweet and dense in B vitamins, very dark organic chocolate is high in antioxidants, and dates are great for feeding our gut biome.

Preparation time: 30 minutes | Serves: 5 or more

WHAT I USE

200g organic mixed nuts

150g organic oats

50g mixed seeds (such as sunflower, pumpkin and sesame)

50g coconut flakes

50g dried banana (make sure there is no added sugar)

10g dried apple

10g chia seeds

10g flax seeds (ground or whole)

10g maca powder

20g raw cacao powder

30g carob powder

Pinch of Himalayan pink salt or rock salt

2 tablespoons extra-virgin olive oil or vegan butter (I use Naturli which is creamy and totally delicious)

2-3 tablespoons coconut butter

3 dates

2 tablespoons coconut nectar or date nectar

400g organic dark chocolate

Cacao nibs or dried raspberries, to decorate (optional)

For the toffee layer (optional)

20 Medjool dates, pitted

Dash of coconut water

HOW I MAKE IT

Put all of the dry ingredients into your food processor. Whizz for a good few minutes until you see the mixture transforming into a powder, and evenly incorporating the cacao and carob. Take the lid off, scrape down the sides then whizz for an extra minute or so.

Next, add the wet ingredients, starting with the oil, coconut butter and dates. Use just enough of the coconut butter so that the mixture starts to bind and clean the bowl. Whizz until you see this starting to happen, then add the coconut or date nectar. If it does not appear to be binding and seems too dry at this point, add a little more oil or coconut butter. The consistency is right when the mixture binds together and begins to form a large ball, soft enough to manipulate. Press with your finger to check this and taste.

Gently press the mixture into a baking tray, forming an even layer. Sometimes I make a thicker base by using a smaller tray, the way my son likes it, or a much larger tray for a thinner base, the way my daughter likes it. Transfer the base to the fridge.

If you want to add the toffee layer, put the pitted dates into the food processor, add a little coconut water and blend for a few minutes until smooth. Dates make the most wonderful toffee which can be used to great effect in a banoffee pie, among other things. Spoon this over the base evenly and put the tray back in the fridge while you make the topping.

Melt the dark chocolate in a small bowl over a pan of simmering water. When it has a smooth consistency, which should take a couple of minutes, pour the chocolate evenly over the toffee layer, or the base, in your baking tray. Spread it into the corners and around the edges with the back of a metal spoon to ensure an even covering. You can now sprinkle a few cacao nibs or even dried raspberries on top. Cut into slices or squares and enjoy! Food tastes so much better when you know what it is doing for your body.

STEP

2

GET YOUR SUBSTITUTIONS IN PLACE

This step is an important part of setting yourself up for success and ensuring that the changes you implement are going to stick. You are not going to change your taste buds overnight, and if you are like most families, you will have had your standard stock of both sweet and savoury snacks that you've now removed as part of the elimination process. So, what do you replace these with?

It is very important that the transition is as positive as possible: the message should be very firmly centred on what you can have, not what you can't have.

If you have it, look back over the last shopping list you made before you started this process. Identify which items are likely to provoke a conversation when they do not appear as usual. For example, as a family, you may have more of a tendency towards sweet or savoury treats or snacks. In my experience the most popular 'backward' choices are usually biscuits and crisps. Poor quality chocolate is nearly always on the list, but if you replace it with the right form of dark chocolate, this food can actually provide antioxidants and boost our happy feelings by increasing our serotonin levels.

Plan to get healthy substitutions ready so that you are prepared for any of those occasions when they may have been eaten, such as after school, in a packed lunch or after dinner.

Find two or three replacements that you and your family can enjoy and stay firm on eliminating everything else. My recipe ideas will help get you started, but there are many other resources out there: it's simply a case of finding a few you can stick to.

It might come as a surprise to you that, in general, we do not need sweet foods in our diet at all. We certainly don't need any extra sugar. So while at first your substitutions might involve making cakes, biscuits, and desserts with healthier sweeteners (see Toolbox), as a rule, you should be working towards minimising these.

CRISPY CHICKPEAS

Not only are these the perfect snack, I have also started making large batches and keeping them in an airtight container to use in meals. We should all be aiming for two or three portions of beans and pulses each day, so this is a delicious and nutritious, not to mention flexible, way to incorporate them into your diet.

Preparation time: 5 minutes | Cooking time: 40-50 minutes | Serves: 4-5 as a snack

WHAT I USE

3 tins of organic chickpeas
Drizzle of extra-virgin olive oil
Rock salt
Black pepper
Seasoning of your choice (try garlic granules, paprika, curry powder, dried chilli flakes, mixed herbs, grated lemon zest, nutritional yeast)

HOW I MAKE IT

Preheat your oven to 220°c fan (if you have an oven with a bottom heated plate, even better).

Empty the tins of chickpeas into a sieve and rinse with cold water. Let them drain a little, then tip the chickpeas onto a baking tray lined with kitchen roll. Dry the chickpeas with more kitchen roll or a clean tea towel by patting and rolling them. Some of the skins will come away here, and this is fine, but leave them in the tray as they will turn deliciously crispy, absorbing the oil and flavouring, and will be the best bit.

Remove the kitchen roll, then drizzle the chickpeas with a thin covering of olive oil. Give the tray a shake to ensure they are all completely covered.

Now you could simply season them with salt and black pepper and put them in the oven, but I like to add extra flavour and nutrients by smothering the chickpeas with nutritional yeast and some dried chilli flakes. You could add herbs, lemon zest, paprika or anything else you fancy!

Put the tray into the preheated oven and bake for approximately 40 to 50 minutes. It will vary according to how dry the chickpeas were and how hot your oven gets. Intermittently throughout the baking time, give them a shake. Turn the oven down to 200°c fan after about 30 minutes as you see them crisping up. Keep moving them around and bringing those around the edges into the centre.

Chickpeas won't go rock hard but you will see their colour and texture change. It's up to you to decide whether they should be on the softer side or much more crispy. My daughter loves these slightly softer, while I love them as crispy as possible, so I take some out for her first and then continue to bake the rest.

These crispy chickpeas make a great base for a tart or a salad topper, but as a snack — perhaps mixed with a bit of chopped red onion and tomato — I can promise you they are not going to hang around your kitchen very long!

CRISPY BAKED CURLY KALE

This is not only my favourite snack but the children's too, and I can never make enough. It goes without saying that everything I use is organic where possible. When we are aiming for optimum health, why would we want additional toxins if we can possibly avoid them? Nutritional yeast adds a savoury, cheesy flavour to crispy kale and is a wonderfully tasty and nourishing addition to your cupboard.

Preparation time: 5 minutes | Cooking time: approx. 25 minutes | Serves: 4-5

WHAT I USE

1 large bag of curly kale
3 tablespoons extra-virgin olive oil
2 large handfuls of nutritional yeast*
Rock salt
Black pepper
Dried chilli flakes, to taste, or another seasoning of your choice (try garlic granules, paprika, curry powder, mixed herbs, grated lemon zest)

HOW I MAKE IT

Preheat your oven to 170°c. Wash the kale then dry it thoroughly with a clean tea towel or kitchen roll. Tear off all the hard stalks until you have only leaves and soft stalks left. Lay these in a large ovenproof dish. Drizzle with the olive oil and rub in the kale with your hands until every piece is covered.

Sprinkle over the nutritional yeast.* Note that nutritional yeast is not the same as brewer's yeast; I use the Marigold brand which can be ordered from Amazon or found in all good health food shops. Rub the yeast into the kale with your hands. Season with salt and pepper then sprinkle over the chilli flakes to taste, or any other seasoning you're using.

Put the kale into the preheated oven and watch carefully to make sure it doesn't burn; open the oven every 10 minutes to shake the dish and move the kale around. After about 25 minutes you should find the kale has crisped up beautifully and absorbed the oil and yeast. Try it to check, and if it's not ready, return it to the oven for another 5 minutes at a time.

Transfer the crispy kale to a serving dish and eat immediately. Enjoy!

SPICY EDAMAME

This isn't really a recipe as such, but a firm favourite in our house as a staple snack. My teens can prepare this themselves in under 7 minutes! Lots of supermarkets now sell frozen edamame if you can't get hold of fresh and it is every bit as good for you, if not better. I would recommend having at least two bags in your freezer at any point to bring out when a quick, warm and nutritious snack is needed.

Preparation time: 5 minutes | Cooking time: 3 minutes | Serves: 4-5 as a snack

WHAT I USE

Edamame, fresh or frozen
Seasoning of your choice (try garlic salt, fresh chillies, lime juice, sesame seeds, fresh ginger, paprika)

HOW I MAKE IT

I would recommend steaming them, if possible, for 3 minutes. After this time, just test one to ensure they are cooked through.

Serve the edamame with toppings of your choice. I love garlic salt, fresh chilli, a dash of lime juice and sesame seeds. But ginger is great too, or a sprinkle of paprika.

This is SO easy to do and ready in under 10 minutes! Have a play with your favourite flavours and enjoy.

NUT BUTTER APPLE SANDWICHES

This is homemade almond butter with fresh apple, which you can make into some tasty sandwiches. Nut butters can be made from your choice of nuts but I love the flavour of roasted almonds which has a wonderful depth. They are also a source of good fats and vitamin E for the skin.

Preparation time: 10 minutes | Cooking time: 20 minutes | Serves: 4-5 as a snack

WHAT I USE

400g almonds

75ml organic extra-virgin olive oil

½ teaspoon ground rock salt

2-4 large tablespoons coconut butter

1 tablespoon coconut nectar or coconut sugar

1 large tablespoon raw cacao powder (optional)

HOW I MAKE IT

Spread the almonds out in a large baking tray, drizzle with the olive oil and sprinkle with the salt. Roast them in a fan oven preheated to 180°c, opening the oven frequently to give them a really good shake and check they aren't burning. Roasting the almonds gives them a wonderful rich flavour but do be careful they don't overcook. This should take about 20 minutes.

Transfer the roasted almonds directly to your food processor or blender and add a tablespoon of coconut butter and the coconut nectar or coconut sugar (these are much healthier, nutrient-dense sweeteners).

Blend the mixture; if it looks dry play around with adding more coconut butter. You may want a touch more salt, or a glug of olive oil. Remember that the nut butter is hot at this stage, and will solidify more as it cools down.

If you wish to turn this into amazing chocolate nut butter, then just add the tablespoon of cacao powder. Again, add more if you fancy it according to taste.

Transfer the finished nut butter to a sealed container and keep it with your other snacks.

Core an apple then stand it up and cut slices approximately 1.5cm wide. Spread a round of apple thickly with nut butter and place a second round of apple on top. Enjoy as a sandwich or slice into smaller segments.

Nut butter is SO versatile. I always have a massive tub on the kitchen counter to use in so many snacks and dishes. It's also delicious, high in protein, nutrient dense and will keep appetites at bay. Great in your smoothies, on top of granola, with desserts and simply on its own. Nut butters are expensive in the shops and it is really easy to make your own. What's more, you can tweak the results to your own tastes. Try throwing some chia seeds in there for extra nourishment and goodness.

STEP
3

PREPARE THE CONVERSATION WITH YOUR FAMILY

If you were to go on a trip with your family, you wouldn't just expect them all to pack, prepare, and get in the car without some consultation, getting their buy-in and perhaps even explaining the rationale behind where you are going.

Changing your and your family's relationship with food is perhaps the most significant journey you are ever going to go on together. It will affect the long-term health and wellness of everyone involved. It may have the ability to protect them from major lifestyle diseases and promote happiness among you all, improving the quality and length of your relationships and interactions.

So, having firmly found your 'why', and become attached to it and what it is going to bring you, it is time to share this with your family.

Find time to have a conversation with them one by one, or all together. A really nice way to do this is while you're all enjoying some absolutely delicious food, which you can use as a prompt for the topic.

Explain what you've decided to do and what this will mean.

Be clear about why you have decided to do it, and share some of your reasons.

Try to explain how it will positively impact everyone in your family, what effect it will have on their lives, both now and in the future.

Stress the benefits, the rewards and the fact that this is an 'upgrade' from what has been happening. Tell them my mantra – 'You Can't Have That, I Love You Too Much' – so they can clearly see that the changes are coming from a place of love, as does all parenting!

Be prepared to answer questions, but stand firm on your decision.

Emphasise the positives behind what you are doing: new upgraded treats, better quality food and less damaging sugars, salts, and empty calorie foods.

Explain the connection food has to some of the things each of them struggles with. It might be their skin, fatigue, digestion, susceptibility to illness, low mood, or anxiety. Or perhaps explain how it will facilitate and support their lifestyle: sport, work and exams, concentration, even leisure time with friends.

Once you've had this conversation, be prepared to revisit it, but remember your values and your 'why' and stay true to them as you overcome any push back or resistance. If you wouldn't let them drink, smoke, or take drugs even occasionally, why would you let them eat damaging foods every day?

Navigate the communication as you see fit and depending on your family's personality and beliefs. My eldest son, for example, still doesn't know the ingredients I put in my alternative chocolate biscuits, or even my chocolate truffles. If he did, I know he might decide not to eat them as he has some limiting beliefs around certain foods. So, I have decided he doesn't need to know. As long as he is enjoying them, that's enough!

BAKED BEANS AND POTATO WEDGES

From being a child who was told (and was afraid it might be true) that I would turn into a baked bean if I ate any more, I have had to develop a more beneficial way to eat my beans. They go so well with oven baked potato wedges, although both of these dishes make great sides for many of the other meals in this book. Where possible, I like to use a selection of good organic potatoes, orange sweet potatoes and purple potatoes if I can get hold of them.

Preparation time: 10 minutes } Cooking time: 30-40 minutes | Serves: 4-5

WHAT I USE

For the potato wedges
7 good-sized potatoes
Olive oil
Rock salt
Ground black pepper
Extra seasoning of your choice
(try garlic granules, paprika,
mixed herbs, chilli flakes)
4 tablespoons nutritional yeast (I
use Marigold)

For the baked beans
½ teaspoon extra-virgin olive oil
1 large clove of garlic, finely
grated
1 red onion, finely chopped
250g (1 carton) passata
1 tin of borlotti beans
1 tin of black beans
1 tin of kidney beans
1 tablespoon Worcestershire
sauce
A good shake of Tabasco
1 tablespoon cider vinegar
1 teaspoon tamari
Small squeeze of coconut nectar
Black pepper, to taste
1-2 red chillies, finely chopped
(optional)

HOW I MAKE IT

For the potato wedges

Preheat the oven to 220°c with the top and bottom elements on if possible. Peel the potatoes if you choose to do so. I often leave the skin on for its nutrient value. Cut the potatoes roughly in half, then half again, then slice into fairly even wedges. You don't want them too small, as they will burn easily, not so large that they don't cook through. Mine are usually 4 to 5cm long and 3cm wide, roughly.

Drizzle a little oil into a large baking tray then sprinkle it with salt and pepper. Space the wedges evenly on the tray and drizzle again with the olive oil. Season the tops and add your choice of extra flavourings. Carefully shake over the nutritional yeast so that they are all evenly covered.

Transfer the wedges to the preheated oven and cook for approximately 30 to 40 minutes, checking them every 10 minutes to move them around and turn them over using a fish slice. Watch those at the edges of the tray don't burn before the middle ones are done.

For the baked beans

About 15 minutes before the wedges are done, put the oil, garlic and onion in a saucepan then gently cook for about 4 minutes until both are soft. Add the passata and stir well. Meanwhile, drain and rinse all the beans in a sieve then leave them to drain again while you go back to the sauce.

Next, add the flavourings: Worcestershire sauce, Tabasco, cider vinegar, tamari, coconut nectar and black pepper. Stir the sauce well and then transfer it to a blender to whizz until you have a smooth purée.

Transfer the sauce back to the pan and then add the drained beans. Mix well to combine. Keep the pan on a very low heat and taste the baked beans to see if you want to add a bit of anything else. If you fancy it a little spicier, add some fresh finely chopped chilli.

Heat through and serve when ready with the potato wedges or absolutely anything else you fancy. They keep well in the fridge for a couple of days, where the flavour only gets better.

Tip: Make a batch at the start of the week and plan your Monday and Wednesday meals around the beans.

HOT PEPPER SAUCE

I make this to pour over roasted vegetables, eat with a homemade tart or to keep in the fridge as a far superior alternative to ketchup.

Preparation time: 5 minutes | Cooking time: 30 minutes

WHAT I USE

2 red peppers (or one red and one yellow), halved and deseeded

3 large cloves of garlic

½ a red onion

4 tablespoons olive oil

4 tablespoons apple cider vinegar

4 tablespoons passata

2 tablespoons tamari

½ a fresh red chilli, chopped (or 1-2 teaspoons dried chilli flakes, depending on how hot you want the sauce to be)

1 level teaspoon paprika

½ teaspoon cumin seeds or ground cumin

¼ teaspoon coriander seeds or ground coriander

Splash of lemon juice

Rock salt and black pepper, to taste

HOW I MAKE IT

Preheat the oven to 220°c fan and lay the peppers on a lightly oiled tray, cut side down. Drizzle olive oil over the top and tuck the garlic cloves, with their skins on, under the halved peppers for protection while they roast. Place the onion half on the tray.

Cover the tray with tin foil and roast the peppers, onion and garlic in the oven for approximately 20 minutes, until you can see the peppers have softened and started to brown on the top.

Meanwhile, add the remaining ingredients to a small blender (I use my NutriBullet).

Take the baking tray out of the oven and transfer the peppers to the blender with tongs or a fork. Squeeze the roasted garlic cloves out of their skins and add to the blender along with the onion.

I like to eat this sauce hot, so I blend it immediately, but you could also wait until the peppers, garlic and onion have cooled. Once thoroughly blended, taste the sauce and adjust the seasoning according to your preference. Store in the fridge where it will keep for at least a week.

MISO HUMMUS

One more super quick idea for snacks that is really nothing new: hummus and crudités! But forget the shop-bought stuff... I'm pretty certain most of you have at least one tin of chickpeas lurking in the back of your cupboard? If you don't have tahini, never mind; I want you to get used to substituting ingredients so you can play around with flavours: try one of the alternative options listed below.

Preparation time: 5 minutes | Serves: 4-5 as a snack

WHAT I USE

2 tins of chickpeas

3 tablespoons (or a healthy glug) extra-virgin olive oil

Lemon juice, to taste (I use about 3 tablespoons as we love it)

1 teaspoon miso paste

1 teaspoon tahini

1 large clove of garlic, grated

Rock salt

HOW I MAKE IT

Drain the chickpeas in a sieve over the sink, then tip them into the blender. Add the oil, lemon juice, miso, tahini, garlic and a really good grinding of salt.

Blitz for 3 minutes or so until the mixture looks creamy and smooth. Taste the hummus and adjust if necessary; you may need more oil, lemon juice or seasoning. Add little by little to get the consistency and flavour that is right for you.

Extras: I will often add an extra ingredient or two to change the hummus up a bit. Miso is one of my favourite ways of adding real depth to this and is of course a gut-nurturing fermented food that I recommend keeping in your cupboard at any time. More often than not I will also add fresh or dried chilli. Roasted beetroot is delicious in hummus, and a swirl of harissa or fresh pesto is another great way of changing it up now and then. You could even use black onion seeds (nigella seeds) which hold a whole host of nutritional benefits, or black garlic.

There's no comparison between homemade and shop-bought hummus, and it takes two minutes to whizz up in your blender. Serve with sticks of carrot and celery, and top your bowl of hummus with black onion seeds, chilli, roasted onion… anything you like. Yummy! I also throw some crispy chickpeas (see recipe on page 64) on top to finish.

CORIANDER PESTO

Fresh pesto takes minutes to make and tastes SO much better than anything you will buy in the shops. I know that so many people look to pasta as a quick answer to a rushed dinner, and if this is the case I always urge them to nourish both the pasta and the sauce, avoiding empty calories. This coriander pesto is my favourite, but of course basil is easily substituted for a more traditional flavour.

Preparation time: 5 minutes | Serves: 4-5 with pasta

WHAT I USE

1 large bunch of coriander

150ml extra-virgin olive oil (use more or less depending on the consistency you want)

2 tablespoons ground almonds (or pine nuts if you prefer, I usually throw these on top)

3 cloves of garlic, peeled and chopped

2 heaped tablespoons grated parmesan (I now use a vegan alternative)

Pinch of dried chilli flakes

Himalayan pink salt, to taste

Splash of lemon juice

HOW I MAKE IT

Simply place all the ingredients in the food processor, and let them work their way into a smooth paste. Taste to check the seasoning and store in an airtight container.

Mix the fresh pesto into nutrient dense pasta — wholemeal, spelt, lentil, chickpea (yes, you can really buy chickpea pasta!) — and add more veggies such as garlic, onions, spinach, mushrooms and chopped tomatoes or your choice of protein.

THE BEST SALAD DRESSING EVER

I don't know about you, but it's salads all the way for at least six months of the year in our house. I think perhaps the most important thing for us is getting the dressings right. My daughter takes a salad of some sort to school every day, so I am constantly making dressings for her to take in a small bottle so the salad won't get soggy. The below is by far our favourite!

Preparation time: 5 minutes | Serves: 4-5 with a salad

WHAT I USE

6 tablespoons organic extra-virgin olive oil

6 tablespoons organic cider vinegar

2 tablespoons sesame oil

1-2 tablespoons organic tamari

1 heaped teaspoon French mustard (wholegrain or Dijon will be lovely too)

1 teaspoon coconut nectar or date syrup

Rock salt, to taste

HOW I MAKE IT

Simply throw all the ingredients into a jug or cup and whisk with a fork until they are combined.

Keep in the fridge to have whenever you need it.

This dressing goes with so many things, so it's easy to ensure you are varying what is in the salad itself. We have such a fantastic variety of leaves, lettuces and different fruits and vegetables to choose from, making it straightforward to get the variety of colour and fibre we need from our foods by throwing in different things each time. Freshly shelled peas, roasted beetroot, toasted seeds and nuts are just a few great options. Whether you have them for a quick lunch or to accompany dinner, salads are the perfect rehydration, and alkalising too.

MAKE THE JOURNEY A FAMILY AFFAIR

As you move further into this programme, I would urge you to keep sharing your new understanding and knowledge, reasons and passion with your family. Note the wins and positive comments you are getting and highlight them to everyone else. Most importantly, try to make your mealtimes as positive as you possibly can to enhance the whole experience of eating better food!

I hope I am not the only one, but that we all have trouble getting our teens, tweens, and children out of their bedrooms, into communal spaces… and into the kitchen. Not only might they be out more than they are in, upstairs more than downstairs and on their phones more than talking to you, but as they get older, the schedules of the combined household are likely to mean that the times you get to eat together are rarer. My house is a prime example of this. As a result, our dinner times have got later and later to accommodate for the fact that I like us all to eat together if at all possible.

These are my top tips to ensure that mealtimes are as positive and family-oriented as possible.

Whenever you can, try to eat when you have the most people home so that it is a 'family affair' and you get to spend positive time together.

Eat round a table so that your body is in a position to digest what you are eating. Make it an event, not a TV dinner or eating on your lap!

Involve the whole family in the planning process each week so that you all feel a shared responsibility for what you eat (see family meal planning below).

Cook together where possible. You could each have different responsibilities, such as who gets the water, cutlery, plates etc.

It might go without saying, but make sure the food is both nutritious and totally delicious. Get to know what foods do for our bodies and tell your family!

Talk about the food and why this is about reward not denial. Good food shared, discussed, and appreciated increases the benefit, as the whole experience is positive.

Limit distractions: make sure the TV is switched off and leave phones in another room on silent so nobody jumps up to answer a call.

Consciously use meal times to connect with one another. Make this a forum for support by sharing your day, thoughts and worries. In our house, we use the phrase 'glad, mad, and sad'. We take turns to share something good about our day, something unexpected or a bit quirky and lastly, anything tough (though this often doesn't happen since the mood is lifted as a result of the first two!)

Enjoy food together and then, as a family, clear away together. Nobody should leave the room until the last bit of clearing away has been done: make this a rule. Their time is not more valuable than yours as a parent. If necessary, allocate different tasks to different people so that even if they are eating separately, they contribute to the experience.

NOURISHED UP MIDWEEK PASTA

Ten minute meals are a must during the busy term time but 'empty calorie' pasta is one of my bugbears! Pasta can be a great fast food but ensure it is made with wholegrains, spelt, vegetables or something that is nutritionally plentiful.

You don't need a recipe for this, so I'm not going to be prescriptive, as we can all boil a pan of water and follow the instructions on the packet to cook pasta (which will vary anyway, according to the shape and what it is made of) and there are literally hundreds of ways for you to combine your preferred veggies and sauces.

For your sauces

Always have a tin of organic tomatoes, passata or even tomato juice at the ready and then 'nourish' the pasta. By that I mean pack it with as many great-tasting veggies as you can. Do this your own way: you could pan fry red onion and garlic, toast some pine nuts, lightly steam broccoli or spinach, and grill sliced mushrooms. A healthy dollop of pesto, a couple of tablespoons of tamari and lots of black pepper with some torn mozzarella thrown in at the last minute, and a dollop of crème fraîche if you choose, is a delicious way to enjoy pasta. Tear up and add a big handful of fresh basil and perhaps olives too, just before serving.

If you are using it, don't forget to let your broccoli sit cut and prepared out of the fridge for 30 to 40 minutes before cooking, or dust it with mustard powder after cooking to get the full benefits of sulforaphane; mustard powder is rich in dietary myrosinase, which can help increase the availability of sulforaphane, particularly in cooked vegetables.

If you have people that won't eat vegetables like this, make a sofrito from onion and garlic in a pan with olive oil. Add peppers, courgettes, spinach, steamed broccoli, even mushrooms too. Let them cook and soften and then add a carton or jar of passata. Transfer to a blender and whizz until smooth. It will look just like tomato sauce and you can add it to the pasta knowing you are pumping it full of veggies that only you will know about!

TOMATO SOUP

Colder weather means comforting soups, and in our house variations on tomato are always the favourite. Soup also means hot and healthy food on the table within 25 minutes, which is all-important when you have three children who are ALWAYS hungry and want food now! Sometimes I use blanched beef tomatoes as the base, but organic tins of tomatoes are also perfect. Adding lentils makes this a filling meal and provides one of your pulse portions for the day.

Preparation time: 5 minutes | Cooking time: 25 minutes | Serves: 5

WHAT I USE

4 tablespoons extra-virgin olive oil

3 cloves of garlic

1 large red onion (or 2 small ones)

1 level teaspoon dried chilli flakes or 1 fresh chilli

3 tablespoons organic red lentils

2 tins of organic tomatoes

1-2 tablespoons tamari

1 tablespoon Worcestershire sauce (I love Lea and Perrins but, since this has anchovy in, I now use a vegetarian version made by Biona)

1 litre vegetable stock (I use one and a half Kallo stock cubes to make the stock for this recipe)

Squeeze of lemon juice

Handful of spinach

1 packet of fresh basil

HOW I MAKE IT

Peel and chop the garlic and onion as finely as you like. In a large saucepan, combine the olive oil with the onion, garlic and fresh chilli if using. Always check how hot the chilli is simply by cutting into it. I run my finger along the flat side of the knife carefully and taste. You can then adapt how much you use depending on who you're cooking for.

Stir the contents of the pan over a medium heat, moving the mixture constantly for 2 to 3 minutes until the onions start to soften, then add the lentils and continue to stir so that nothing burns or sticks to the bottom. If you're using dried chilli flakes, add them now.

After a further 3 minutes or so, add the tomatoes, tamari, and Worcestershire sauce. Stir well then pour in the stock and add a squeeze of lemon juice. Let the mixture gently come to the boil.

Leave the soup to cook for about 10 minutes, then stir in the spinach and the basil. Immediately take it off the heat, as you want to retain all the fresh goodness of the spinach without overcooking it.

With a small hand blender, whizz the mixture in the pan until it is smooth but still wholesome and thick. Decide whether you would like to add more liquid at this stage.

Season the soup to taste and serve immediately. A swirl of crème fraîche is a good contrast with the chilli. Great served with Eskimo slippers and underfloor heating!

THE BEST NUT ROAST EVER

People think of nut roast as the archetypal standard for vegetarian food. As such, it is often reproduced in pubs and the frozen food counters of supermarkets as a pretty tasteless option which feels like a poor second to the meat roast. I have played around with my recipe over the years and it's always my favourite thing on the plate, replacing the stuffing for a meat roast, and is a winner for any diet!

Preparation time: 5 minutes | Cooking time: 35-40 minutes | Serves: 4-5

WHAT I USE

1 tablespoon avocado or olive oil

1 large red onion, roughly chopped

3 cloves of garlic, sliced

5 chestnut mushrooms, sliced

3 large handfuls of mixed nuts (I include almonds, walnuts and Brazil nuts as standard but anything else is a bonus!)

2 slices of good organic bread

Splash of lemon juice

1 teaspoon mixed herbs

1 teaspoon paprika

1 tablespoon tamari

3 tablespoons passata

1 tablespoon Worcestershire sauce

Shake of Tabasco sauce

Rock salt and black pepper

HOW I MAKE IT

Preheat the oven to 180°c. Drizzle your baking tray with oil so the nut roast doesn't stick.

In a frying pan, gently sweat the onion, garlic and mushrooms in the oil for just a couple of minutes. Transfer them to the food processor, add the nuts and bread then gently pulse to just combine but no more.

Add the lemon juice, herbs, paprika, tamari, passata, Worcestershire sauce, Tabasco and seasoning to taste. Gently pulse the mixture once more, scraping the sides down with a spatula to ensure the consistency is uniform throughout. You don't want to create a purée though, as a bit of texture is important.

Transfer the mixture to your baking tray and mould it into a loaf shape. Pop a foil cover over the top and bake the nut roast in the preheated oven for approximately 25 minutes.

The nut roast can be taken out now and saved to heat through when needed, or you can take the foil off and put it back in the oven for a further 10 to 15 minutes to finish cooking. You want the top to go crunchy, but be careful not to let it burn.

Serve generous slices with delicious miso gravy (I make mine with cornflour) and all your roast accoutrements! Enjoy any day of the week.

MUSHROOM, BUTTERNUT AND TARRAGON RISOTTO

I can't tell you how delicious this is. It looks so impressive yet is simple to make. The secret is not to leave the pan once you get going; don't let anything stick by adding stock bit by bit every few minutes and turning the risotto over continuously. Make sure you keep tasting it to add the flavours you want more of at the end. Make this dish your own!

Preparation time: 10 minutes | Cooking time: 25 minutes | Serves: 6

WHAT I USE

8 dried porcini mushrooms

200g butternut squash, peeled and cubed

1 head of broccoli, broken into florets then quartered

Olive oil

1 large red onion, finely chopped

6 large chestnut mushrooms, quartered

500g organic arborio risotto rice

1 heaped tablespoon organic bouillon (I use Marigold)

4 tablespoons lemon juice

2 heaped teaspoons dried tarragon (fresh would be even better if you can get it)

1 litre boiling water

50ml Oatly cream or 1 large tablespoon crème fraîche

Handful of parmesan, grated (you can use a vegan hard cheese with a tablespoon of vegan cream cheese instead, I use Violife)

Rock salt and black pepper

HOW I MAKE IT

First, soak the porcini mushrooms in a bowl of boiling water for 15 minutes to rehydrate them. Keep the stock this makes for later!

Steam the cubed butternut squash for just a few minutes to soften it slightly, then do the same with the broccoli, testing after just a couple of minutes. Set aside for later.

Put a good glug of olive oil in a large pan. Add the onion and cook on a low to medium heat until translucent. Add the chestnut mushrooms and cook for a couple of minutes, ensuring there is enough oil in the pan. Add the rice and stir well to cover the grains evenly with the oil. Do this for 3 to 4 minutes until the rice is translucent.

Make up a litre of stock by adding the bouillon, lemon juice and tarragon to the boiling water. Stir it well. You will probably need more water but start with this and your porcini stock. Slowly add them to the pan bit by bit and keep stirring. This is the part where you cannot leave the pan and must keep turning over the contents. Keep adding liquid until the rice is cooked but not stodgy. Al dente is perfect at this point.

Gently fold in the porcini mushrooms, steamed broccoli, butternut squash, crème fraîche or Oatly cream, and parmesan or vegan alternatives. Taste the risotto; if you need a little more lemon juice or tarragon, add it now. Season well with plenty of black pepper.

Serve the risotto with a sprinkle of parmesan or vegan hard cheese. I will often leave the butternut out and make a mushroom risotto, on top of which I place tomatoes roasted in balsamic vinegar: a nice alternative for you to try.

HAVE YOUR 'RUSH NIGHT' MEALS AT THE READY

However well you plan, there will always be those nights when you won't be there and you need really good, healthy staples to fall back on. This means finding healthier alternatives for takeaways, ready meals, and white 'empty calorie' pasta.

Over time, you'll find your own quick meal ideas. But to get you started, here are a few of my favourites:

Homemade beans and baked sweet potatoes

Simple baked salmon and roasted veggies (easy to do in one tray together or in parcels of greaseproof paper or plant-based salmon substitute, see page 98)

A really good pasta (spinach, spelt, wholewheat, seaweed, lentil etc.) with an easy passata sauce and any veggies left in your fridge

Stir fry: use spelt or wholewheat noodles, a range of veggies and a simple, sugar-free sauce made from a little pressed apple or orange juice and tamari

A veggie burger, or plant-based sausages with couscous and salad (try out a few burger brands and find one you like. Some of the best ones I have found are made by the supermarket themselves. You can't beat Waitrose vegan leek sausages right now)

A Spanish omelette pepped up with a little chilli

A huge salad with beans and pulses and avocado covering all the food groups and served with a delicious dressing (see recipe on page 78)

Another trick for tackling 'rush nights' is to make sure you have some of your ingredients and meals prepped already. Here are some ideas that I've found that help me stay 'on top':

When cooking rice, make a batch. You can put some in the freezer or in the fridge for later that week. When you come to use it, rinse it thoroughly with plenty of boiling water.

Peel a batch of potatoes a few days in advance and leave them in water in the fridge. When you're ready to use them, rinse and prepare as usual.

Pre-prepare salad and keep it in a sandwich bag for when you need it quickly.

Keep a jar of homemade salad dressing in the fridge.

Make a batch of pasta sauce, smuggling in a range of veggies, blend it until smooth and then freeze it in ice cube trays. You can then pop them out as and when you need them.

Keep a range of dips in the fridge – I like homemade hummus, smashed avocado or guacamole, homemade salsa, and homemade raita – to accompany more basic meals.

Batch cook meals and keep them in the freezer (more on this in Step 7).

Get your kids to help you prepare (peel, chop or freeze) your vegetables for the week so that all you need to do is take them out each time you need them!

Make more food than you need so that on the nights you really can't face cooking or it is impossible, you still have home-cooked food to enjoy.

If you are going to be home late, ask your partner and/or children to get the ingredients out and half-prepared by the time you get home (or vice versa if someone else is cooking) e.g. onions chopped, potatoes peeled, herbs and spices at the ready.

Plan a meal swap with a friend: you both cook up a double batch and then swap so that you have two meals covered.

There are also some great brands out there offering more nutrient-dense ready meals for nights when you know you won't have time to cook. If you stock up on them in advance, you won't have to resort to second-best alternatives. Explore these options, and don't forget to read the labels!

FLEXITARIAN SKEWERS WITH BBQ SAUCE

This is a really easy meal to flex any way you like and again you don't really need a recipe, just an idea for what to use!

Preparation time: 10 minutes | Cooking time: 25 minutes | Serves: however many you want

WHAT I USE

Mushrooms

Pepper

Tomatoes

Courgettes

Onions

Fresh pineapple

Organic chicken breasts

Halloumi/tempeh

For the BBQ sauce

200ml passata

2 tablespoons apple cider vinegar

2 tablespoons tamari

2 teaspoons date nectar

½ teaspoon smoked paprika

1-2 cloves of garlic, grated

Squeeze of lemon juice

Dash of Tabasco

Good shake of Worcestershire sauce

HOW I MAKE IT

Make colourful veggie skewers with a selection of mushrooms, peppers, tomatoes, courgettes and onions, or whatever you want to include. I also use fresh pineapple if I have it.

Then separately prepare organic chicken skewers. Simply cut the meat into roughly 4cm cubes and thread these onto the skewers. Do the same for the halloumi skewers.

Make the sauce by mixing all the ingredients together, then taste and adjust to how you like it. Drizzle some over the skewers (keeping enough to serve them with) then place them on separate baking trays.

Cook the skewers in the oven at 180°c for approximately 20 minutes, ensuring they do not burn. When everything is cooked through, take them out and drizzle each skewer with the remaining sauce. Serve with buckwheat, couscous, potato wedges or brown rice. So quick, so easy, so delicious… and healthy!

SUPER QUICK NOURISHED UP COUSCOUS SALAD

I prefer to use giant wholemeal couscous than the finer white stuff we see everywhere. Simply follow the instructions on the packet to cook and then pack it out with finely chopped vegetables and salad of your choice. Season well and add lemon juice.

Here are some ideas I love for this meal:

Roasted peppers, parsnips and courgettes

Chopped onions

Chopped tomatoes

Grilled halloumi

Vegan Greek cheese

Chopped cucumber

Chopped mint

Chopped parsley

Olive oil

Chopped spinach

Crispy fried tofu

CRISPY COATED TOFU STIR FRY

In our house we don't really like tofu. However, crispy tofu is something of a revelation and I was told it tasted better than crispy chicken! That's some accolade from my boys. Here I used breadcrumbed tofu from a brand called Tofoo, whose tempeh I am also loving. Delicious, nutritious, plant-based wholefood heaven! Flex this up with crispy chicken if you choose or any meat of your choice.

Preparation time: 15 minutes | Cooking time: 10 minutes | Serves: 5

WHAT I USE

2 packets of breadcrumbed tofu

½ large head of broccoli, broken into florets and sliced

Sesame oil

10 chestnut mushrooms

4 cloves of garlic, finely chopped

3cm ginger, grated

2 medium-size carrots, cut into fine batons

2 handfuls of cashew nuts

½ a red and ½ a green chilli, finely chopped

½ teaspoon Chinese five spice

1 large red onion, sliced

1 red, yellow or orange pepper, deseeded and sliced

½ a medium-size courgette, sliced

1 lemon, juiced

4 tablespoons tamari

4 tablespoons orange juice

Dash of Tabasco

Dash of date nectar

100ml passata

Handful of spinach

Handful of fresh coriander

HOW I MAKE IT

Firstly, I rinse some brown basmati rice and put this into a pan of boiling water to cook, but you could serve the stir fry with noodles if you choose. Meanwhile, cut the tofu into small squares or slices.

Lightly steam the sliced broccoli for just a few minutes until it softens a little. In a hot pan with a little sesame oil, fry the tofu until crispy. You might need to do this in two batches so the pan isn't crowded. Keep the cooked tofu warm under tin foil.

In a larger pan, fry the mushrooms, garlic, ginger, carrots, cashews and chillies in a little oil. Add the Chinese five spice too and mix well. As the mushrooms soften, throw in the onion, pepper, steamed broccoli and courgette.

To make the sauce, add the lemon juice, tamari, orange juice, Tabasco, date nectar and passata to the pan. Mix through, taste, and adjust as necessary.

Add the spinach and fresh coriander at the last minute. You want it to wilt but not get soggy. Serve the stir fry immediately on the bed of rice or noodles, placing the crispy tofu on top.

If you are unable to find breadcrumbed tofu in the shops, simply coat some plain tofu yourself. Prepare a plate with a couple of tablespoons of cornflour, a tablespoon of sesame seeds, some ground rock salt and black pepper mixed together. Slice or cube the tofu and press each piece into the flour mixture to coat evenly before frying.

CHILLI TOFU OR SALMON RAMEN

This meal is super quick to prepare and. in our house, eaten super quickly too! Full of crisp veg and just as hot as you like it with fresh chilli, it is also rich and fragrant with fresh coriander, lime leaves and lemongrass. Go plant-based with cashews and marinated tofu, or even my 'not salmon steaks' (see recipe on page 98), or poach salmon fillets in the broth while it cooks.

Preparation time: 5 minutes | Cooking time: 15 minutes | Serves: 4-5

WHAT I USE

1-2 teaspoons coconut oil

3 cloves of garlic, very finely sliced

1-2 fresh chillies, diced

3cm ginger, grated

2 kaffir lime leaves

1 stick of lemongrass, left whole

1 red onion, finely sliced

1-2 red or yellow peppers, deseeded and sliced

6 brown mushrooms, sliced

1 teaspoon shichimi (Japanese spice blend)

1 litre hot water

1 teaspoon organic miso paste

2 limes, juiced

1 tin of coconut milk (400ml)

1 packet of tofu or 4-5 salmon fillets

Handful of cashew nuts

Noodles of your choice (I love Clearspring Organic)

Bunch of fresh coriander

HOW I MAKE IT

Put the coconut oil in a large saucepan on a medium heat. Add the garlic, chilli and ginger. Stir while they cook for a few minutes, then add the kaffir lime leaves and lemongrass to the pan. Cook for another minute or so. Add the onion, peppers and mushrooms and continue to stir well. Add the shichimi and mix so the spices are distributed evenly.

Make up about a litre of stock with the hot water and miso paste. Stir in the lime juice, then add it all to the saucepan. Open the tin of coconut milk and empty it into the pan, stirring as you go.

Next, add your tofu, cut into cubes or slices, and cashew nuts (or salmon fillets). Cook for about 4 minutes, then taste the soup and check for any seasoning that needs to be adjusted.

Prepare the noodles of the choice while the tofu or salmon is poaching. I like to cook them in the broth as it really thickens up, but you may prefer to cook them separately in boiling water.

When the noodles are cooked, you are ready to serve the ramen immediately. Divide it between bowls and top with generous amounts of fresh coriander and chilli to your own tastes.

BAKED ATLANTIC SALMON/ NOT SALMON WITH GINGER, LIME, CHILLI AND TAMARI

This is my daughter's absolute favourite meal, so much so that she reproduced it for a recent school 'masterchef' assessment and won! She also finished half an hour before everyone else: double win. In terms of dinner on the go and the quickest meals, this is a champion. I've been making a plant-based version for myself lately and have created a 'not salmon steak' which works so well in terms of texture and flavour absorption.

Preparation time: 10 minutes (salmon) 20 minutes (not salmon) | Cooking time: 15 minutes | Serves: 4

WHAT I USE

Olive oil

Two handfuls of spinach

4 fillets of Atlantic salmon

3 cloves of garlic, grated

5cm ginger, grated

2 fresh chillies, finely chopped, or 1 teaspoon dried chilli flakes

3 or 4 large limes, juiced

4-5 tablespoons tamari

1 bunch of coriander

For the 'not salmon steaks'

2 large cauliflower heads, very lightly steamed

½ a packet of tempeh, chopped into small pieces (about a small handful)

½ a tin of jackfruit

Rock salt and black pepper

HOW I MAKE IT

If you are making the plant-based version, set about making the 'not salmon' first. Simply place all the ingredients for the 'steaks' in a food processor and pulse very lightly just once or twice, until the mixture is combined but no more. You still want the different textures and pieces visible. Scoop the mixture out with your hands, about a quarter at a time, and form it into 'steaks' before laying on to an oiled baking tray, with the spinach as a base.

Preheat the oven to 200°c. Drizzle a baking tray lightly with olive oil and layer the spinach on top. Skin and wash the salmon fillets, then lay them on top of the spinach.

Spread the garlic, ginger and chilli evenly over the salmon. Pour the lime juice over all four fillets, followed by the tamari. Add half the coriander to the tray, then drizzle a little more olive oil over everything.

Cover the tray with foil and bake in the preheated oven for 10 minutes. Remove the foil and bake for a further 5 minutes until the salmon or 'not salmon steaks' are fully cooked.

Serve immediately with the rest of the fresh coriander, plenty of fresh vegetables and your choice of accompaniment. I love this with wild rice but quinoa or buckwheat is equally nourishing. You can use any type of salmon in this recipe, or indeed substitute it for a tuna steak. Dinner done and delicious in less than 25 minutes!

PLAN YOUR FAMILY DINNERS

The advice I give here is all about planning your meals for the week. You aren't going to be able to change everything you eat overnight, but these smaller steps should help to make your changes sustainable.

NOURISH UP YOUR FOOD

Start by making healthy additions to the foods you are eating already. This is what I call 'nourishing up your food'. For example, if you are cooking pasta, you will probably have already upgraded the pasta that you use from white to wholewheat or similar. The second stage is to see what you can add to boost the nutrient value and move your family towards their ten a day. So for a pasta dish, choose good-quality protein, but then pack the meal with as many vegetables as you can. Use passata instead of a shop-bought sauce and add flavour to it yourself with store cupboard staples such as Worcestershire sauce or fresh herbs. For a side dish, perhaps add a salad or two to three more veggies.

ADD IN NEW ELEMENTS

Next, change up parts of a meal you are all used to with new ingredients you maybe haven't tried before, maximising the veggies, and gradually introducing new foods alongside those that are more familiar. Use flavours your family like and are used to, but find better ways of delivering them. To do this, get inspired by taking time to browse areas in the supermarket you may not have done before, go to a food market or flick through food magazines and recipe books to take inspiration from those ideas. When I changed my recipes to entirely plant-based, it was all done on familiar territory: same recipes but with a change of protein, not a huge remove from what my family are used to. It also means you are less likely to end up with a meal that no one likes because it is so different.

ADD NEW MEALS ALONGSIDE FAVOURITES

Every week, try an entirely new meal idea. This is where you really start to build a new repertoire! Go by the 50% rule of how to build your plate and use good quality ingredients in combinations that excite you and your family. You could join a Facebook group to inspire you, such as my 'Eat Nourish Flourish' community, buy a new recipe book or two, listen to podcasts, follow chefs on Instagram… In addition, plan a family night where everyone enjoys a 'nourished up' version of a favourite dish. In this house it's homemade pizza or nachos loaded with homemade salsa, guacamole, and raita!

KEEPING EVERYONE HAPPY

You're likely to be dealing with a number of different requirements. But whatever mix you are of vegans, pescetarians, vegetarians and meat-eaters, it is all totally workable. Start by planning a main meal that is predominantly plant-based, and you can then begin to dress or accompany it with the other proteins that satisfy each diet.

The science and latest evidence has convinced me that a plant-based diet offers us the best protection from lifestyle disease and the greatest chance of healthy longevity. And in the long term, I'd advise getting yourself somewhere on the flexitarian spectrum. Your family may not move at the same rate as you, or indeed you at the same rate as them, but this is about being informed about your choices while you move to a healthier lifestyle. It may be that you decide you never want to cut out meat and that is your choice, but understand what you are eating, source your ingredients carefully, and embrace the differences in your family.

COCONUT, BUTTERNUT, LIME AND CHILLI SOUP

I can't tell you how good this is!

Preparation time: 5 minutes | Cooking time: 15 minutes | Serves: 4-5

WHAT I USE

2 medium-size red onions, finely chopped

2 tablespoons olive oil

Pinch of dried chilli flakes or ½ a fresh red chilli, finely chopped

1 whole butternut squash, peeled and diced into 2cm cubes

1 litre stock (I use Marigold)

1 tin of coconut milk (400ml)

2 limes, juiced

Rock salt and black pepper, to taste

Good handful of chopped coriander

HOW I MAKE IT

In a medium-sized saucepan, cook the onion in a little olive oil over a medium heat until translucent. Add the chilli and stir again.

Meanwhile, place the cubed butternut squash in a steamer above boiling water and cook for just a few minutes so it softens but doesn't become soggy.

Add the squash to the onions and stir well, then pour in the stock and coconut milk. Add the lime juice and season to taste with salt and pepper.

Cook the soup on a low heat for 10 minutes, then add most of the coriander, leaving a little to top the soup with as you serve it.

At this point, I use a hand blender to whizz the soup in the pan until it has a smooth consistency with no lumps. Be very careful not to splash yourself with boiling soup! You can of course wait until it cools and transfer to an upright blender, but be very careful doing this with hot soup.

Reheat if needed and serve immediately with a scattering of seeds or crispy chickpeas on top along with the remaining coriander.

HOMEMADE PIZZA

I'm going to invite you to Saturday pizza night, the healthy way. It's much more fun (admittedly more mess too) and a surefire way of getting your teenagers to stay in for the night and creating a party atmosphere. To say this is my boys' favourite meal is an understatement!

Preparation time: 20 minutes | Cooking time: 5-10 minutes | Serves: 4-5

WHAT I USE

For the dough

2 tablespoons olive oil

600g spelt flour

Rock salt and black pepper

2 heaped teaspoons baking powder

½ teaspoon garlic granules

½ teaspoon dried chilli flakes

1 teaspoon paprika

For the tomato sauce

Generous glug of olive oil

Dash of lemon juice

1 teaspoon grated or finely chopped garlic

Pinch of rock salt

750ml lovely organic passata

HOW I MAKE IT

The oven needs to be super hot, so put it on at 230°c about half an hour before you want to cook the pizzas, with heat from the bottom element if possible.

For the dough

Mix the olive oil with a little tepid water. Place the flour in a bowl, season it with salt and pepper, then add all the remaining ingredients except the liquid. Stir to distribute all the spices evenly. Add the water and oil mixture little by little until it just binds the mixture, then knead with your hands until the dough cleans the bowl but isn't sticky. Simply divide the dough into balls to make the number of pizzas required. So for five people, make five balls of dough.

For the tomato sauce and toppings

I make extra sauce so we can have it on top of the pizzas when they are done, the way calzone should be. Simply stir the oil, lemon juice, garlic and salt into the best passata you can find.

On a chopping board, prepare all the toppings. This is your choice entirely. Some of the toppings we use are olives, fresh tomatoes, mozzarella, vegan mozzarella, red onion, garlic, basil, broccoli, spinach, capers, raisins, pine nuts, chicken, mushrooms… you get the idea!

In my house, once everything is ready I throw flour over the surfaces, get the rolling pins out and the family do the rest. I also prepare a number of large pieces of greaseproof paper, carefully floured so the pizzas don't stick.

Decide whether you'd like a calzone or standard pizza, roll out the ball of dough then top or fill the pizza base with a nice covering of tomato sauce and toppings. Bear in mind that the more toppings you put on, the longer the base will take to get crisp. Place the pizza or calzone carefully onto a piece of floured greaseproof paper, then whack it in the hot oven. I don't have a proper wooden paddle but my fish slice does the trick just as well. Watch carefully until the pizza is done to your liking, then serve immediately, with extra tomato sauce on the table for the calzones and a huge salad.

FAMILY NACHOS OR FAJITAS

A plate of nachos always goes down well whatever the day or situation! I've been lucky enough to find vegetable tortilla chips at my local Co-op, but also like to make my own for a healthier way of indulging. They are topped with salsa and guacamole, which you can easily make yourself and are perfect for making fajitas with too: just add the chilli (see recipe on page 114) and some wraps to make a brilliant DIY dinner.

Preparation time: 20 minutes | Cooking time: 20 minutes | Serves: 4-5

WHAT I USE

For the tortilla chips

1 large sweet potato

2 parsnips

2 large beetroot

3 tablespoons olive oil

Seasoning of your choice (try salt, pepper, paprika, onion salt or nutritional yeast)

For the salsa

2 tins of organic chopped tomatoes

3 tablespoons extra-virgin olive oil

2 tablespoons lemon juice

3 spring onions, finely chopped

1 large red onion, finely chopped

2 large cloves of garlic, finely grated

½ a medium hot chilli, finely chopped

Large handful of fresh coriander, finely chopped

For the guacamole

2 large ripe avocados

1 tablespoon olive oil

1 clove of garlic, finely grated

½ a chilli, chopped

1 lemon, juiced

4 cherry tomatoes, finely chopped

Small handful of fresh coriander, finely chopped

For fajitas

Tortilla wraps

Chilli (see page 114)

HOW I MAKE IT

For the tortilla chips

Preheat the oven to 165°c. Peel and very thinly slice the sweet potato, parsnip and beetroot with a large sharp knife or a mandoline. Then lay them out in a single layer on a baking tray sheet lined with greaseproof paper, drizzle with oil, season them with your choice of flavourings and pop the tray into the preheated oven to bake for about 20 minutes, at which point they should be ready for turning over. You should only need to do this once but check the chips regularly for colour while you make the accompaniments.

For the salsa

Simply empty the tinned tomatoes into a large bowl, add the olive oil and lemon juice, then stir through the onions, garlic, chilli and coriander. If you like a smoother consistency, whizz the salsa with a hand blender for about 30 seconds.

For the guacamole

Scoop out the avocado flesh, roughly chop it and then mash the pieces together with a fork to your preferred consistency; I like to leave a few chunks. Add the olive oil, grated garlic, chilli and lemon juice to the avocado. Season and mix well. Lastly, stir through the chopped tomato and coriander. Taste the guacamole and adjust the seasoning as needed.

When the tortilla chips are done, allow them to cool and then top generously with the homemade salsa and guacamole. Cheese is a great addition and I use a lovely plant-based pre-grated version from Violife. I've also used jalapeños, fresh coriander, olives, red onion, and if you fancy turning it into more of a meal, tear some cooked chicken over too! I love marinated jackfruit on my nachos so flex it both ways.

For fajitas

Pile some of the chilli into soft tortilla wraps, top with the salsa and guacamole, then roll up and serve with homemade tortilla chips on the side. As with the nachos, you could add grated cheese of your choice, fresh coriander, sliced red onion, jalapeños and sour cream (or a vegan alternative) to the fajitas before rolling, or whatever you and your family fancy!

MUSHROOMS AND/OR CHICKEN IN LEMON AND ROSEMARY

This incredibly simple yet delicious and impressive dish is absolutely full of flavour and ticks all the boxes for a satisfying, healthy and filling meal. You can serve it with rice as suggested below, roasties (as an alternative Sunday lunch) or pack a healthier punch with mixed grain quinoa or even bulgar wheat. I love the healing qualities of shiitake so use them whenever I can, but it's your choice whether or not to include them, as with the chicken.

Preparation time: 10 minutes | Cooking time: 20-25 minutes | Serves: 4-5

WHAT I USE

4 tablespoons organic lemon juice

1-2 teaspoons bouillon (I use Marigold)

1 tablespoon finely chopped fresh rosemary

300g rice (I like a mixture of brown basmati and wild rice)

3-4 tablespoons olive oil

2 large organic chicken or turkey breasts (optional)

15 brown mushrooms, quartered

6 shiitake mushrooms, halved

2-3 tablespoons crème fraîche (I love the Oatly version)

HOW I MAKE IT

Prepare any vegetables you want to accompany the meal and set to one side (broccoli and carrots add great colour to this dish).

Boil a kettle and prepare the stock by adding the lemon juice, bouillon and rosemary to 425ml of hot water. Stir and leave to infuse.

In a medium saucepan, heat the water for the rice, adding a dash of lemon juice and a dash of olive oil. Wash the rice in a sieve and when the water has boiled, add it to the saucepan and leave to cook on a low to medium heat.

Add some olive oil to a large frying pan over a medium heat. If you are including the meat, neatly slice the chicken or turkey breasts from end to end, approximately 1cm in width and 3 to 4cm in length. Add them to the pan. Keep turning the slices over for 2 minutes or so until lightly cooked on all sides, when the meat has just turned white. Add the mushrooms and stir for a further 3 minutes or so. I usually make two pans of this dish side by side; one with organic chicken and one simply with mushrooms.

Add the stock, stir it through and turn the heat up. Cook until the liquid has reduced by approximately half and started to thicken slightly. This will take about 15 minutes, but keep an eye on it and don't let it reduce to nothing; everyone will want as much of this sauce as they can get! If the sauce doesn't thicken as much as you would like it to here, stir a teaspoon of cornflour into a little cold water to make a paste, then stir this into the pan.

Put the prepared veg in the steamer when you are 5 minutes away from completion, and check the rice. Take the chicken and/or mushroom mixture off the heat and scrape any stuck on bits from the sides of the pan into the sauce for maximum flavour. Stir through the crème fraîche, then serve the dish immediately with the rice and vegetables.

HALFWAY CHECK

When you've worked through about six of the steps, I would like you to take stock of where you are on your journey. Your learning so far will have been vast. This is a chance to stop, take a breath and a short break, shore up your reserves, strengthen your thinking, assess who you may need more help from…and then continue on your way. Think of it like an extra reality check:

Look at your original Ultimate Goal. How do you feel when you read it again?

Are you still as connected to it as you were at the beginning, or do you need to rewrite/tweak it?

Are you consciously or subconsciously going against your own plan?

Are you still clear on your values and why you started this in the first place? Do they hold strong?

What limiting beliefs are popping up from time to time? Are you counteracting them with something more positive? How?

What difficulties or obstacles are you encountering from other contextual factors, such as people, work, unforeseen circumstances?

How are you dealing with the obstacles?

Most importantly, what have been your big wins so far?

What have you learned about yourself, food and your family by this point?

There are many reasons why people can suddenly stall on their coaching goals – including self-sabotage – but this exercise isn't about excuses or knuckle-rapping. It's about raising your awareness, noticing how you are feeling, knocking out those limiting beliefs, and replacing them with beliefs that will serve your goal and help you move forward. Go over your weekly 'wins' and notes about what you've learned. No doubt you will surprise yourself when you see just how different your life already is.

Believe
YOU CAN,
and YOU are
HALF WAY
there

BATCH
COOKING

I am a huge fan of batch cooking for so many reasons, and I love empowering my clients to use this technique. It not only frees up your time, but it provides you with valuable support when you're facing pressure. It's all about working smarter, not harder, and reaping the rewards.

Put simply, batch cooking means making far more than you are going to need or consume in one sitting. As a result, you can compensate for those times when you are time-poor without compromising on food quality. I'm yet to find a meal that I am not able to make more of or pack into lunchboxes the next day for the children.

This will involve a few simple steps to start with:

Adapt your shopping lists to allow you to cook larger quantities of the same thing. Good things to start with are a basic ragu, a variety of veg-packed soups, or paella made with nutrient-dense rice and nourished up with veggies, proteins, and even pulses.

Have your storage containers at the ready – you might need to buy more – and clear out your freezer so you have space to fit them when needed.

Make sure you have cooking pans big enough to make large batches of sauces and foods.

Find times when you can prepare some food in advance for later, but also get used to making double the amount you normally do.

This might require a mental shift so that, in your mind, you're now cooking for six instead of three, for example, but it will start to make your life so much easier that you could soon be cooking for the 5,000 and loving it!

The best recipe to get you started with batch cooking is a basic ragu that you know your family will enjoy. Ragu can easily be converted for any diet (I use organic soya and jackfruit, but you may wish to use turkey mince) and easily adapted; that could mean four or five meals for your week already sorted, if it comes to it. There really are so many possibilities. And your ragu can be kept frozen so it's ready and waiting for those 'rush nights' – bonus!

5 MEALS FROM 1 RAGU!

This is a base recipe that will convert to at least four family meals. It's one of my easiest dinners, which I use as my go-to whenever I need food ready double quick with the least hassle.

You can sub the soya mince for turkey, chicken or beef mince if preferred. I often use a tin of jackfruit, well broken up.

Preparation time: 10-20 minutes | Cooking time: 20-25 minutes (for the ragu base) } Serves: 6

WHAT I USE

Oil of your choice

1 large red onion

3 cloves of garlic

½ a red pepper

½ a green or yellow pepper

1 small courgette, finely chopped

7 brown mushrooms, quartered

3 large handfuls of soya mince (approx. 150g)

1 tin of chopped tomatoes

Good glug of passata

2 tablespoons tamari

2 tablespoons Worcestershire sauce

1 tablespoon paprika

2 teaspoons lemon juice

½ teaspoon miso paste

Pinch of mixed Italian herbs

For chilli

1 tin of kidney or mixed beans

½ teaspoon dried chilli flakes

1 teaspoon fajita seasoning (optional)

For lasagne/moussaka

2 tablespoons cornflour

600ml milk (dairy or plant-based)

200g grated vegan cheese

Handful of nutritional yeast

1 packet of organic egg-free lasagne sheets

1-2 large handfuls of spinach

1 large aubergine, sliced

HOW I MAKE IT

Put a little oil in a large pan. Peel the onion and garlic, chop them finely then add to the pan and cook for a few minutes. Deseed and chop the peppers, then add them with the courgette and mushrooms. Stir well and add the soya mince. If you're using meat, you may want to cook this first before the onion and garlic to brown it. Note that I use the soya you rehydrate, which is why I measure in handfuls. Add all the remaining ingredients for the base to the pan. Stir well and leave to cook for about 15 to 20 minutes. Taste the ragu and adjust the seasoning, then serve as one of the following meals.

For bolognese, simply serve the ragu with a nutrient-dense pasta such as wholemeal, spelt, chickpea, lentil or pea pasta.

For shepherd's pie, place the ragu in a medium-size ovenproof dish and top with either mashed potatoes (sweet and white both work, or you could use a mixture) or sliced potatoes, then bake in the oven until piping hot and golden on top. You could even try mashed swede for something different.

For chilli

When you add the tomatoes and other ingredients to the ragu, leave out the Italian herbs but stir in the beans, chilli and fajita seasoning if you are using it. Serve the chilli with rice and some fresh coriander, guacamole (see page 106), natural yoghurt or Oatly crème fraîche if you like.

For lasagne

While the ragu is cooking, combine the cornflour with just enough olive oil to make a smooth paste in a small pan over a medium heat. Add the milk gradually, stirring constantly and quickly, until you have a silky smooth sauce. Season well, add the grated cheese with a little nutritional yeast and stir until melted. Layer the ragu with the lasagne sheets, spinach and béchamel sauce in an ovenproof dish, sprinkle a little vegan cheese and a shake of nutritional yeast on top, then bake in the oven until piping hot and golden.

For moussaka

While the ragu is cooking, pan fry the slices of aubergine in a little oil and make a béchamel sauce (see the lasagne method above). Layer the ragu with aubergine and béchamel in an ovenproof dish, then bake in the oven until piping hot and golden on top.

AUBERGINE ROGAN JOSH, BUTTERNUT SQUASH ALOO AND RAITA

I tend to make some sort of curry at least twice a week. Not only do I adore the flavours, but the inclusion of garlic, fresh turmeric, herbs and spices makes them an immune-boosting choice.

Here, I've paired two dishes plus a raita. I absolutely love using cashews in curries as they add such great texture. It means that if you are used to eating meat, you really won't miss it!

Preparation time: 15 minutes | Cooking time: 40-45 minutes | Serves: 4-6

WHAT I USE

For the rogan josh

1 large aubergine, diced into 3cm cubes

1 medium red onion

2 cloves of garlic

1 level teaspoon each of fenugreek seeds, paprika and garam masala

½ teaspoon each of cumin seeds and ground turmeric

Couple of cardamom pods

½ a red or green chilli or ¼ teaspoon dried chilli flakes

1 tin of chopped tomatoes

Splash of lemon juice

Dash of tamari

For the butternut aloo

½ a butternut squash

3 white potatoes

1 large onion

2 cloves of garlic

2cm fresh ginger

1cm fresh turmeric or 1 teaspoon ground turmeric

1 red chilli

2 tablespoons coconut oil

1 heaped tablespoon curry paste

1 teaspoon nigella seeds

1 green pepper

200ml passata

Good handful of cashew nuts

2 large handfuls of spinach

1 bunch of coriander

HOW I MAKE IT

I highly recommend Patak's range of pastes (not sauces) which are flavourful and a great tool for cooking quickly and healthily. At any given time, I have the rogan josh, korma, masala and tikka pastes in my fridge to mix and match, creating a different curry each time.

Peel the butternut squash and potatoes for the aloo, then chop them both into 2cm cubes. Steam the cubes until still firm but softening slightly. Meanwhile, finely chop the onion, garlic, ginger, fresh turmeric and chilli for the aloo then preheat the oven to 170°c.

In a large pan on a medium heat, add a good glug of olive oil and the aubergine for the rogan josh. While it softens, finely chop the onion and garlic, then add them to the aubergine after about 8 minutes. When they are translucent, add the spices and chilli. Cook for another minute or so until well mixed, then add the tinned tomatoes, lemon juice and tamari. Taste and season with rock salt and black pepper if necessary. Stir well and then transfer the rogan josh to an ovenproof dish. Pop this into the preheated oven while you continue making the aloo.

In the same pan you were using for the rogan josh, add the coconut oil, onion, garlic, ginger, turmeric and chilli for the aloo. Keep stirring to prevent the garlic from sticking or burning. Next, add the curry paste, any other spices you are using and the nigella seeds. Deseed and chop up the green pepper, add it to the pan and keep stirring.

Next, stir the passata into the aloo to create a sauce. Season with salt and pepper then taste and add lemon juice for tartness or tamari for richness if needed. You might also want to add a little water. When you are happy with the sauce, add the butternut squash, potatoes and cashews. Cook the aloo for about 15 minutes on very low heat. Finally, chop the spinach and coriander then stir them through until just wilted.

Just before the curries are ready, make a quick raita. Combine four tablespoons of yoghurt with about half a grated cucumber, a grated clove of garlic, a dozen chopped mint leaves, a splash of lemon juice and a pinch of salt. Taste and adjust the seasoning, then serve alongside the rogan josh and butternut aloo.

THAI RED CURRY

I am easing my children into a more plant-based diet, so at the moment I cook a vegetarian meal and then add something extra for them. For example, prawns simply turned over in a hot pan immediately before serving can be added to this curry when dishing up. The below is just some guidance; be creative with the veggies you want to use. The sauce is so delicious that anything in it will be transformed anyway!

Preparation time: 10 minutes | Cooking time: approx. 20 minutes | Serves: 5

WHAT I USE

Coconut oil
2 large cloves of garlic, grated
4cm fresh ginger, grated
2 lemongrass stalks
2 lime leaves
Fresh chilli or dried chilli flakes, to taste
1 heaped teaspoon good Thai red curry paste
1 teaspoon organic vegetable bouillon (I use Marigold) or 1 stock cube
1-2 tins of coconut milk
200g creamed coconut
2 teaspoons coconut nectar (or sweetener of your choice)
2 limes, juiced
Handful of cashew nuts
6 large brown organic mushrooms, quartered or halved
6 salad potatoes, quartered
½ a red pepper, sliced
½ a yellow pepper, sliced
Handful of baby corn
Handful of mangetout
½ a head of broccoli, finely sliced
Bunch of fresh coriander, to serve

HOW I MAKE IT

First, briefly steam the salad potatoes because they won't soften up enough in the pan. In a large pan for the curry, start to cook the garlic and ginger in a teaspoon of coconut oil, taking care they don't burn and stirring constantly.

Add the lemongrass, lime leaves, any chilli, the curry paste and stock. Keep stirring while gradually adding the first tin of coconut milk. This is your base.

To this, add the creamed coconut, coconut nectar and the juice of the two limes. Taste the sauce and season appropriately. Next add the cashews, mushrooms and steamed potatoes.

Let them cook for approximately 5 minutes before adding the peppers, baby corn and mangetout. You want to keep these as crunchy as you can to maintain the goodness. Lastly, add the broccoli. Now decide whether you have enough sauce, and add some or all of the second tin of coconut milk if necessary.

Stir through and cook for no more than a few minutes. The last thing you want is soggy vegetables! Serve the curry immediately on a bed of brown rice and scatter copious amounts of coriander over the top.

BUTTERNUT STEAKS WITH FETA, TAPENADE, RED ONION AND BASIL

This dish is extremely versatile and you can interchange the butternut with turkey steaks, or even a piece of fish. There are multiple ways to flex this dish.

Preparation time: 5 minutes | Cooking time: 25-25 minutes | Serves: 5 or more

WHAT I USE

5 slices of butternut squash, cut widthways approx. 1cm in depth or an alternative base of your choice

1 small jar of black olive tapenade

1 large red onion, chopped very finely

2 tablespoons sliced black olives

3 tablespoons chopped fresh tomato

1 packet of feta (or a plant-based equivalent)

2 tablespoons pine nuts

Spoonful of homemade pesto (optional, see recipe on page 76)

Squeeze of lemon juice

Avocado or olive oil

Rock salt and black pepper

Large handful of basil, finely chopped

HOW I MAKE IT

Preheat the oven to 180°c and lightly coat a baking tray with oil. Lay your 'bases' of choice in a baking tray with a thin covering of oil. If you are using butternut squash, ensure your slices are not too thick or they just won't cook through. You may even want to pop them in the oven covered with foil for 10 minutes before adding toppings.

Using a teaspoon, put a dollop of tapenade on each base and spread it out to cover the top well. Add the chopped red onion, olives, and fresh tomato.

Next, break up the feta or alternative using your hands, which is so much nicer than cutting it into cubes. Sprinkle it over the base with the pine nuts and, if you fancy, dot a bit of pesto here and there. Drizzle the topped bases with a little lemon juice and a little avocado or olive oil. Season with salt and pepper to taste.

Cover the tray with foil and bake in the preheated oven for around 25 minutes. Check after 10 and 20 minutes. Add the basil towards the end of the cooking time, leaving enough to sprinkle over just before you serve up.

This is delicious served with sweet potato wedges, mixed quinoa grains or mixed grain rice. Ensure you accompany it with a huge salad or fresh green vegetables too!

LUNCHES

Heating up meals from the night before for the next day's lunches is my trusted way of sending my teens to school knowing they have something hot, delicious, and nutritious. There are some wonderful snack and food pots available out there that will keep food fresh and warm for hours. They also wash extremely well and go in the dishwasher (though you might want to avoid glass flasks in case of breakages).

Sandwiches are deserving of a special mention here as they are so often the 'go-to'. Personally, I believe that we have far better options available to us, and my family has reached a point where we hardly eat any bread at all. But that's not to say sandwiches can't also be 'nourished up':

Upgrade your bread to wholemeal, sourdough, rye, buckwheat, or spelt: in short, anything wholegrain. Look for seeded varieties, or even search out easy healthier bread mixes so that you can make it yourself, if you like. You must still check the labels, though. So much of the bread available today contains about 26 ingredients. You should be looking for something that contains the minimum amount. Three would be perfect! Remember that bread usually contains yeast which can upset our gut balance and cause candida (yeast overgrowth) so just be aware of this. Soda bread is often a good choice and various mixes are available which are super simple to make yourself.

Add salad, olives, vegetables, hummus, guacamole, and other puréed dips if possible. A traditional sandwich is approximately 70% bread: make sure you add in enough veggies to swing the balance back to that 50%. Be mindful of this when preparing and maybe make an extra salad to eat alongside, or a huge glass of tomato juice.

A time-saving tip is to make your sandwich fillings the night before. Prep them and leave in the fridge ready to finish off quickly in the morning.

Here are a few other lunch ideas:

Salads. Again, you can make the components the night before, but take your dressing separately so that it doesn't make your salad soggy by lunchtime. You can have a batch of dressing in the fridge ready to decant when needed.

Soups. Homemade soup, just heated the next morning and popped in a thermal snack pot, is a real winner. Even better is miso soup – which can be made from a wonderful fermented paste in less than 2 minutes – mixed with a sprinkling of seaweed (a true superfood) and spiced up with Tabasco and Worcestershire sauce. Tofu is a wonderful addition to this.

Crudités and homemade hummus

Fresh fruit and homemade nut butter

My personal favourite on-the-go meal is an avocado and a pot of homemade crispy chickpeas.

BEETROOT TIKKI

When I cook, I usually have an idea in my head of what I want to do. I may then look at a couple of other recipes and have a play, which is exactly what I did here. If you lack confidence when it comes to experimenting with food, this recipe is a great place to start because there are so many spices to adjust, and doing that will help you get used to swapping ingredients in and out.

Preparation time: 25 minutes | Cooking time: 10 minutes | Serves: 4-5

WHAT I USE

3-4 large beetroot, peeled and quartered

3 large potatoes, peeled and chopped

2 slices of good brown bread (I actually had beetroot bread!)

1 teaspoon ground coriander

1 teaspoon chaat masala

1 teaspoon mango powder (amchur) or lemon juice

1 teaspoon ground fennel seeds

½ teaspoon red chilli powder or cayenne pepper

½ teaspoon garam masala

¼ teaspoon ground turmeric

1 green chilli, finely chopped

1 teaspoon ground or freshly grated ginger

1 teaspoon black salt or rock salt

2 tablespoons cornflour or rice flour

2 tablespoons olive oil

HOW I MAKE IT

Preheat the oven to 200°c and roast the beetroot in a little oil, lemon juice and seasoning. This will take about 20 minutes. At the same time, steam the potatoes until they are cooked but not soggy.

Place the beetroot and potatoes in a large bowl. Separately, soak the bread in water then squeeze the excess out completely: you do not want this mixture to be too soggy. Put the slices into the bowl with the vegetables, then add all the spices, chilli, ginger and salt. Combine everything well with your hands, or pulse just a few times in a food processor to form a pliable mixture, then shape this into round patties.

Put the cornflour or rice flour on a plate with some seasoning. Place each patty into the flour and turn gently to ensure that they are evenly coated on all sides.

In a pan, heat the olive oil then fry the patties (you may need to do this in batches) until they turn crisp and golden. Place the cooked patties on a plate lined with kitchen roll so any extra oil is absorbed.

Serve the beetroot tikki hot with any chutney, dip or sauce of your choice. I made a plant-based yoghurt raita with onion, mint and cucumber: you could try the recipe on page 116.

BAKED AVOCADOS WITH HALLOUMI OR TOFU

Avocados are incredible, and one of the only 'complete' foods we can eat, offering our bodies everything we need in the way of nutrients. While I love avocados any which way, this recipe is just heavenly. If you have never baked them before, I urge you to give them a go. Play around with ingredients as usual and find your own way, but this is a great base to start with.

Preparation time: 10 minutes | Cooking time: 35 minutes | Serves: 4

WHAT I USE

4 avocados

1 packet of halloumi or tofu, diced into 1cm cubes

1 red onion, finely chopped

10 cherry tomatoes, very finely chopped

3 tablespoons chopped mixed nuts or pine nuts (walnuts are especially delicious in this)

1 small red chilli, chopped

Handful of basil, chopped

Good glug of olive oil

Splash of lemon juice

Sprinkle of nutritional yeast

Rock salt and black pepper, to taste

HOW I MAKE IT

Preheat the oven to 180°c. Halve the avocados, take out the stones then carefully scoop out the centres, leaving the skins intact. Dice the avocado flesh and put this in a bowl. Put the skins onto a baking tray.

Add all the other ingredients to the bowl of avocado and simply mix together until everything is well combined. Divide the mixture between the skins, not worrying if they overflow a bit! Give each one a healthy shake of nutritional yeast to ensure the topping will be crispy and delicious.

Cover the stuffed avocados with foil and pop into the preheated oven for 15 to 20 minutes. Take off the foil and bake for a further 5 minutes until you can see the top has browned. Enjoy immediately with steamed vegetables or a fresh salad!

CRISPY TOFU OR HALLOUMI SALAD WITH MANGO AND PASSION FRUIT

This is a salad that I used to make with halloumi, pairing the saltiness of the cheese with the distinctive tart flavour of passion fruit. But I now replace the halloumi with crispy coated tofu and it works every bit as well. It's so quick, but also really filling so you don't need anything else to go with it. I make this for two people and we are happily stuffed!

Preparation time: 5 minutes | Cooking time: 5 minutes | Serves: 2

WHAT I USE

1 packet of tofu or halloumi, sliced or cubed

Drizzle of sesame or olive oil

Green salad leaves of your choice (I use watercress which is slightly peppery, and spinach which is the perfect background to these flavours)

½ a cucumber

1 large ripe mango

3 passion fruit

Handful of toasted sesame seeds

Crispy Chickpeas, to throw on top (see recipe on page 64)

HOW I MAKE IT

Lightly cook the tofu in a pan over a medium heat, adding a dash of sesame oil which gives it a wonderful flavour, and turning the pieces so each side gets a bit of colour. Alternatively, do exactly the same with the halloumi, for which I usually use olive oil rather than sesame.

Simply arrange the salad leaves on a plate, then chop or slice the cucumber and place the pieces around the edge of the plate. Peel the mango and cut into slices approximately 1.5cm wide, then arrange them as you see in the photo.

If you like, toss the green salad in a dressing of your choice. I used a date nectar and tamari dressing on page 78, and for this recipe I usually add a little orange juice which complements the flavours beautifully. Lay the warm tofu or halloumi on top, halve the passion fruit and scoop out the centres, distributing them liberally across the salad.

Sprinkle the salad with the sesame seeds and as many crispy chickpeas as you like. Enjoy!

SAUSAGE & BLACK BEAN CASSEROLE

So good I was asked by the children to make it twice in one week! There are so many brilliant things about this dish, not least that it's perfect warming winter food, but the fact that it can be prepared in approximately 30 minutes has to shout 'make me' even on evenings when we are tired or overstretched. It is exactly the type of meal perfect for batch cooking (see page 112) and therefore a quick hot lunch on the trot the next day for you or the family. I often serve it with a pile of green vegetables, including broccoli and peas, next to heaps of creamy mashed sweet potato.

Preparation time: 10 minutes | Cooking time: 25 minutes | Serves 6

WHAT I USE

1 packet of plant-based sausages

1 teaspoon vegetable bouillon

Splash of red wine

1 large red onion

3 cloves of garlic

2 tablespoons red lentils

1 level teaspoon shawarma spices (a Middle Eastern mix you can buy)

½ teaspoon paprika

Fresh chilli or dried chilli flakes, to taste

1 tablespoon tamari

½ tablespoon Worcestershire sauce (I use a vegan version)

Good shake of Tabasco

2 tins of organic chopped tomatoes

½ a red pepper, sliced

1 tin of black beans (I use Biona Organic)

Handful of fresh parsley, roughly chopped

HOW I MAKE IT

Cook the sausages under the grill, until they are nicely browned on all sides, then preheat the oven to 200°c. Stir the bouillon into 285ml (half a pint) of hot water and add the wine.

Meanwhile, chop the onion and garlic then put them in a casserole dish with a dash of oil to cook gently for a few minutes. Add the lentils and stir really well, not letting them stick to the bottom, for a couple of minutes.

Next add the spices, tamari, Worcestershire sauce and Tabasco. Mix well before adding the prepared stock and then the tinned tomatoes.

Stir everything together before adding the pepper and black beans. Finally, chop the sausages into thick rounds and add to the casserole. Give everything a really good stir, then place the casserole in the oven for 30 minutes to finish cooking and bring all the flavours out.

Take the casserole out and serve immediately with a handful of spinach to really nourish this up, along with the parsley and even a swirl of plant-based cream to finish.

This is great with mash or hasselback potatoes, which you can make by slicing almost through a baking potato repeatedly from one end to the other, so you have lots of deep slits about half a centimetre apart. Place on a baking tray, drizzle with olive oil, season and sprinkle with nutritional yeast or any herbs and spices of your choice, then roast at 200°c in a fan oven. They take about 30 to 40 minutes depending on the size and how crispy you like them.

STEP
9

DRINKS

There is only ever one all-day drink for me and that has to be water. Our bodies can go without food for a while, but water is a different matter; by the time you are thirsty, you are probably already dehydrated. Up to 60% of the adult human body is water and according to H.H Mitchell, Journal of Biological Chemistry 158, the brain and heart are composed of 73% water and the lungs are about 83% water. Think of water as the biggest treat you can give yourself: it cleanses the body, plumps the skin, and replenishes the cells. I visualise the body as a long muddy river full of dirt and rocks that need to be cleared, and as I flood it with fresh water, I nourish and cleanse the river, clearing it of impurities and obstacles.

Here are a few tips for how to drink more water and other ways to 'nourish up' what you drink:

Drink a litre of water while you exercise, and then fit in another four or five glasses throughout the day.

Boost the flavour of your water using fresh fruit or herbs. Try adding a slice of orange, strawberries, lemon balm or even basil to your water glass or bottle. I like to mix plenty of mint with lemon or lime and cucumber and, in the summer, I fill a large cooler with flavoured water so that it's on tap for the whole family.

Switch it up with naturally carbonated water and find a natural sugar-free cordial.

Swap milk for delicious, plant-based alternatives (see How to Stock Your Cupboards on page 165). Just don't expect your tea or coffee to taste exactly the same! There will be a transition period as you get used to the different flavours.

If you drink alcohol, choose clear spirits. Vodka and gin are far kinder on the system, in particular the liver, and easier to process than wine and beer. But if you don't drink, don't start. Alcohol does us no good.

There are some wonderful infusions and healing teas out there. Experiment with herbal, green, matcha and white teas and find a new favourite.

Try kombucha and kefir. They taste great – when you get used to them – and have been used throughout the centuries for their gut-friendly and immune-supporting properties.

Have a good drinking yoghurt once a day to help keep your gut healthy, or add it to your smoothie. I use a plant-based alternative.

Blend your own milkshakes. I use plant-based milks and make anything from banana to chocolate shakes, adding in ground nuts for extra protein and texture.

Choose pressed juice. Tomato is one of my favourites and it helps me get in another portion of veggies each day. As a general rule, avoid juices that are from concentrate because they usually contain lots of extra sugar.

Switch to organic coffee. A cup or two a day can have benefits, but only if it is organic. Non-organic coffee is exceptionally high in pesticides used to preserve the crops.

ICE LOLLIES

Not a recipe as such, but a reminder that it is so easy to make your own ice lollies in the summer months, and how much healthier they are than most shop-bought varieties!

At any point during the summer, I will keep coffee in the fridge, made with any combination of plant-based milks and a good spoonful of plant-based vanilla ice cream. Simply pour this mixture into moulds; a few cacao nibs sprinkled in make this even more special. The ice cream ensures the liquid doesn't separate as the mixture goes into the freezer partially frozen already.

Fruit lollies are easily made by blending blueberries, strawberries, banana, mango and yoghurt with coconut water and almond milk, then poured into moulds and frozen. They are absolutely delicious but also get so many portions of fruit into you, in the most refreshing way possible!

Again, a good tip to ensure they do not separate is to keep the fruit in the freezer prior to making the lollies. I usually break up two or three bananas and put them into freezer bags ready, along with keeping a couple of bags of mixed fruit and berries in the freezer too.

You could even adapt my smoothie recipes (see pages 58 and 136) into lollies; add more fruit than veg just this once!

The simplest of all would be banana lollies: just the peeled fruit whizzed up with your choice of dairy-free milk and frozen to enjoy on a hot day.

SUPER GREEN SMOOTHIE

Everywhere you go at the moment there is a 'super green' smoothie on the menu. Green stuff can be full of phytonutrients and can alkalise your body (imagine this as calming everything down; disease thrives in acidic conditions). I make my usual fruity morning smoothie then have this mid-morning. Do experiment with throwing different things in but I'm loving the following recipe, which makes one full NutriBullet-sized blender jug.

Preparation time: 5 minutes | Serves: 2

WHAT I USE

Handful of kale
2 broccoli florets
3cm fresh ginger root
1cm fresh turmeric root
¼ cucumber
6-8 large mint leaves
Juice of 2 large limes
1 kiwi, peeled (optional)
1 apple (you can peel if you choose, I do to make it a little less bitty)
1 teaspoon chia seeds
Pressed apple juice
Coconut water

HOW I MAKE IT

Simply place all the ingredients in the blender and then whizz up with a mix of apple juice and coconut water; work out the balance of liquids according to how sweet you want the smoothie to be. Two thirds apple juice and one third coconut water works well for me.

Great for managing stress levels and keeping your body on an even keel. Go Green!

BANANA MILKSHAKE

This is a firm favourite in our house any time of the year. Full of protein and filling, it is a five minute quick fix for hunger and tastes totally delicious, while nourishing our gut health at the same time.

Preparation time: 5 minutes | Makes 3 large milkshakes

WHAT I USE

2 large bananas
2 tablespoons mixed nuts or ground almonds
1 teaspoon chia seeds
Milk of your choice

HOW I MAKE IT

The type of milk you use here is down to you. I use a mix of almond, oat and coconut, measured out using one of the glasses I want to serve the milkshakes in. I tend to use just over a litre of milk for three drinks.

Then, simply put the peeled bananas, nuts, seeds and milks into the blender and whizz until smooth. Throw in some ice before or after and drink immediately!

You could also add half an avocado before blending, which makes it creamy and suitable for any lunch replacement. A wide range of plant-based milks are now available, so you could experiment with a mixture of almond, oat, coconut, soya, rice, hazelnut, hemp and others.

CHOOSE
AND COOK
YOUR FOODS
BY COLOUR

Colourful fruits and vegetables are better for your immune system and are anti-inflammatory because they contain more nutrients, antioxidants, and phytochemicals (these are unique to plants and associated with a wide range of health benefits) so the more colours on your plate, the better! That's why the expression 'eat a rainbow' has become commonplace.

Next time you're faced with a choice between a variety of fruit or veg with colour and a variety without – red onions, brown mushrooms, red cabbage and red grapes over the white varieties or red pears over green – pick the colourful option. This is an exceptionally easy way to add nourishment to your diet without changing the foods and flavours you are used to.

You can also use this principle to start experimenting with foods you haven't tried before. Aim for a minimum of four colours on your plate and try to increase it every week. You could even have a family competition to see who can eat the most colours in a week, depending on your children's ages of course!

Don't leave out the greens, though. It is vitally important to regularly eat cruciferous vegetables too, so include broccoli, spinach, kale and greens in your meals. Green vegetables are alkalising and calming for the body. Asparagus has even been linked to lowering anxiety because it contains chromium, and asparagus extract has been approved by the Chinese government as a natural functional food for this purpose.

In addition to colour, diversity in the vegetables you are eating is also extremely important. This is vital for a healthy gut biome to support our immunity, and the billions of microbiota that populate the gut, our second brain. There is constant communication from our gut to our brain via our vagus nerve, as our biome produces neurotransmitters. Each vegetable we eat provides its own biome, and therefore its own properties, so in order for us to function optimally we need this huge variety to be working together and balancing one another. 90% of our serotonin is manufactured in the gut, so this has a significant impact on our mental wellbeing too.

The bottom line is that these foods give us the fibre we need to feed our 'friendly' bacteria, which then reward us with short chain fatty acids that in turn support excellent colon health.

BEETROOT AND EDAMAME RISOTTO

There's not much to say about this except WOW! It's so good, in fact, that the first time I made it, I was asked to make it again the very next day. Beetroot is a really good source of iron (which can be a pick-me-up and give you some energy) and naturally occurring folic acid. It also contains nitrates, betaine, magnesium and other antioxidants. All that aside, it tastes amazing when roasted and combined with the right flavours.

Preparation time: 5 minutes | Cooking time: approx. 50 minutes | Serves: 5

WHAT I USE

500g brown risotto rice

3 medium beetroot, peeled and chopped into eighths

4 tablespoons olive oil

Rock salt and black pepper

1 large red onion

1 litre bouillon stock (I use Marigold)

3 tablespoons lemon juice

1 tablespoon chopped rosemary (dried is fine if you don't have fresh)

1 small bowl of edamame beans (I shucked them from a bag of frozen pods, but you can buy them prepared or even substitute with peas if you can't get hold of edamame)

1 packet of feta cheese (or a vegan equivalent)

HOW I MAKE IT

A note on the main ingredient: My slight issue with risotto was that the rice is always a refined white, and therefore not a 'wholefood'. However, I recently discovered brown risotto rice and I'm loving it. As always, have a play with ingredients to suit your personal tastes.

You can soak the brown risotto rice overnight, in which case it can go straight into the pan, but I always forget to do this in advance so my first step is to boil the rice for about 25 minutes, or until it has softened but still has a good bite. At the same time, preheat your oven to 220°c.

Put the beetroot on a baking tray, drizzle with a little olive oil and season with salt and pepper. Cover with foil and roast the beetroot in the preheated oven for 25 minutes. When done, carefully chop the beetroot into bite-size pieces (roughly 0.5cm cubes) and set aside.

Chop the onion very finely and add to a large pan with a really good glug of olive oil. Cook until the onion begins to turn translucent. Add the prepared rice, and stir to coat in the oil before starting to add the stock, with the lemon juice and rosemary stirred in, bit by bit. Allow the rice to absorb the liquid before adding more and keep the risotto moving to ensure it doesn't stick.

When the rice is nearly cooked, stir in the beetroot. If you need to add more liquid to finish cooking the rice then do so, or you may not need all the stock.

Stir through the edamame beans or peas right at the end so that they are heated through but not overcooked. Heap the risotto onto plates and sprinkle with feta or your choice of vegan equivalent. I serve this with a gorgeous salad too. Enjoy... I'm pretty confident you will!

MIXED ROASTED VEGETABLES WITH CANNELLINI BEANS, HOMEMADE MISO HUMMUS & HOT PEPPER SAUCE

You know by now that I don't prescribe to the idea of a recipe you stick to exactly. I like you to play around with ideas, adding your own flavours and combinations. Your kitchen isn't mine and the ingredients you have, from size to colour, will be different too, so nothing is exact anyway. I change the roasted vegetables I use every time I make this dish, and urge you to mix and match with those you prefer.

Preparation time: 20 minutes | Cooking time: 30-40 minutes | Serves: 4-5

WHAT I USE

For the roasted veg and beans

2 large sweet potatoes

¼ small butternut squash

2 large purple beetroot

2 smaller yellow beetroot

½ a bulb of garlic

½ a head of cauliflower, broken into large florets

1 large red onion, quartered

Extra-virgin olive oil

1 teaspoon dukkah or other seasoning (I used paprika, mustard powder and a pinch of Cajun spices)

Rock salt and black pepper

2 tins of cannellini beans (borlotti would also work)

1 tablespoon lemon juice

For the hot pepper sauce

See recipe on page 74

For the miso hummus

See recipe on page 75

HOW I MAKE IT

Preheat the oven to about 210°c with the fan and bottom plate on, if possible. Meanwhile, prepare your veg. Peel the sweet potatoes and butternut squash, then chop the flesh into 4cm cubes (deseeding the squash as you go if needed). Peel both types of beetroot and chop them into 3cm cubes; they are denser than squash and potatoes so should be smaller. With a sharp knife, slice the top and bottom off the garlic bulb so all you have to do is squeeze the garlic out when roasted. If you don't do this now you'll have trouble extracting the piping hot garlic later!

Lay all the vegetables, including the cauliflower and red onion, in a baking tray and drizzle generously with olive oil to ensure they are all covered. Sprinkle over your seasoning (dukkah or another blend of your choice) and rub in or toss to coat all the veg. If you don't have any spices, just salt and pepper will do because the hot pepper sauce will provide flavour.

Cover the tray with foil and pop into the preheated oven. You can roast the peppers for the sauce at the same time. Meanwhile, empty your beans into a pan and add a generous glug of olive oil and the lemon juice. Season well with salt and pepper. Don't turn on the heat yet as they will only take a couple of minutes to warm through.

Take this time to make your hummus according to the recipe on page 75.

After the vegetables have been roasting for about 30 minutes, take the foil off and check them. They should be nearly done. Take the peppers for your sauce out of the oven and put them into a small blender jug. Make the sauce according to the recipe on page 74.

Turn the heat on for the beans and take the rest of the veggies out the oven. Finely chop half the roasted onion and squeeze two cloves of the roasted garlic with the chopped onion into the beans. Stir well, heat through and taste. Adjust the seasoning if necessary.

Plate up a big swirl of hummus topped with two spoonfuls of beans, then arrange the roasted vegetables on top. Drizzle hot pepper sauce around the edge of the plate with extra on the side. I also like to sprinkle over some roasted chickpeas to finish.

EXOTIC MUSHROOM AND JACKFRUIT TART

Exotic mushrooms such as shiitake, maitake and reishi have long been used to support good health. I buy at least one packet of shiitake and one packet of mixed mushrooms a week on top of my chestnut mushrooms. I have also started making my own pastry and I love the results. We all tend to think the process is too time consuming, but actually you can make and bake the pastry case in as little as half an hour.

Preparation time: 25 minutes | Cooking time: 40 minutes | Serves: 4-5 (makes 2 medium tarts or 1 very large tart)

WHAT I USE

For the pastry
400g organic spelt flour
200g cold vegan butter, diced into 1cm cubes
Rock salt and black pepper
A little ice cold water

For the filling
Handful of dried porcini mushrooms
A little olive oil
1 large red onion, peeled and chopped
3 large cloves of garlic, peeled and chopped
1 tin of jackfruit
250g mixed mushrooms
100g chestnut mushrooms
2 tablespoons lemon juice
Dash of miso paste
1 teaspoon Worcestershire sauce (I use Biona as not all brands are vegan)
1 heaped teaspoon chopped fresh rosemary
1 tablespoon crème fraîche (I use Oatly)

Optional
2 large organic chicken breasts
Handful of Crispy Chickpeas (see page 64)

HOW I MAKE IT

For the pastry

Preheat the oven to 175°c. Grease and flour the dish(es) you will be using for your tart(s). Put the flour into a large bowl, add the cubes of cold vegan butter, then season with a little rock salt and black pepper. With clean hands, start to rub the butter into the flour by rubbing it between your fingers until you have something that looks like a bowl of fine breadcrumbs. Then add tiny amounts of ice cold water at a time to bind the mixture together.

If you are doubling up to make two tarts, split the dough in half and roll out each piece on a floured surface to make the cases. Transfer carefully to the prepared dishes and trim off any extra pastry that overhangs the edges, patching up any holes with the excess. Cover the pastry with greaseproof paper, fill with baking beans and blind bake in the oven for about 20 minutes. Meanwhile, make your filling.

For the filling

Soak the porcini mushrooms in a small amount of boiling water for a few minutes. Meanwhile, heat the olive oil in a pan, add the chopped onion and garlic, then gently cook until translucent. If you are making a chicken filling, slice and add it to the pan at this stage until almost cooked through.

Add the jackfruit and all the mushrooms to the pan. Cook for a further 3 minutes or so before adding the lemon juice, miso paste, Worcestershire sauce and fresh rosemary.

When they've had 20 minutes, take the tart cases out of the oven, remove the baking beans and greaseproof paper, then pop them back into the oven for a further 10 minutes before removing once more. Add Crispy Chickpeas to the baked tart cases if using.

Stir the crème fraîche through your filling(s) and spoon into the baked tart cases. Place the tart(s) in the oven for a final 10 minutes. Serve immediately with Hot Pepper Sauce (see page 74) which goes really well with this, and a crisp green salad.

THE HEALTHY
SNACK
CUPBOARD

This step is different from substitutions, but just as necessary. As well as having your 'go-to' snacks at home, you'll want to get into the habit of taking food with you so that you don't have to resort to junk under pressure or when offered. This is where I put all the 'extras' that my teens take with their packed lunches. It includes shop-bought products that will add nourishment to their diets, so we can give these to others and eat them ourselves with a clear conscience.

What you choose to have in your snack cupboard will be down to you and your family's tastes and habits, but here are some of the things I have at the ready to be eaten in moderation, when you cannot make all your snacks yourself from fresh ingredients:

Mini packets of dried fruit

Nuts (allergies allowing)

Dried edamame beans (though make sure you check the label carefully: many contain added sugar)

Fruit purées ('squeezies')

Apple or fruit crisps

Shop-bought snack bars (but again, make sure you check the labels since many so-called 'health bars' are anything but!)

Mini coconut water cartons

Seaweed crisps

Roasted seeds

Mini almond milk cartons

Nut butter pouches

Salted broad beans

Salted corn

Chickpea and mixed grain crackers (we love the Rude Health brand products)

Organic dark chocolate rice cakes

There are even much better crisp-style snacks available now, made with lentils, vegetables or quinoa. But my advice as ever is to check the labels, make sure you understand what all the ingredients are, avoid yeast and hidden sugars which can be listed under a myriad of names, and minimise salt. Stick to rock salt in these products if possible. Ideally, they should have very few ingredients and no fillers, additives, or preservatives.

It goes without saying that you'll want to keep a full and varied fruit bowl in your kitchen alongside the healthy snack cupboard. In addition, a fridge full of vegetable crudites will help you reach your ten a day, and keep you all going until mealtimes.

RAW CHOCOLATE TRUFFLES

Boasting vitamins E and B, antioxidants, good fats and the 'happy feeling' generator, serotonin!

Preparation time: 10 minutes | Serves: 4-5 as a snack

WHAT I USE

300g ground almonds

2 heaped tablespoons carob

1 tablespoon cacao or cocoa powder, plus extra for coating

1 ripe avocado

2 pitted dates

A little date syrup or coconut nectar

HOW I MAKE IT

Simply blend all the dry ingredients together in the food processor, then add the avocado flesh, dates and syrup or nectar. Whizz until the mixture is smoothly blended and well bound; it should form a ball and clean the bowl. Adjust the consistency by adding date nectar if the mixture is too dry, and more carob or almonds if it looks too wet.

Roll pieces of the mixture between your hands to form small balls, approximately 3cm in diameter. Roll the truffles in cacao powder and place them in a bowl in the fridge to keep them fresh. Enjoy.

BREAKFAST FLAPJACKS

While I call these breakfast flapjacks, I will eat these as a snack post-work out or mid-afternoon if I feel my energy is low, because the oats provide long-lasting, slow-releasing energy. Quantities really don't have to be exact here as it depends on what size trays you have and how much you want to make. I always make a huge batch that will last the week for five of us.

Preparation time: 5 minutes | Cooking time: 20 minutes | Serves: 5 or more

WHAT I USE

265g organic oats

50g mixed nuts, chopped

20g mixed seeds, including chia and linseed

20g raw cacao nibs

200g vegan butter

50ml organic coconut nectar or date nectar

HOW I MAKE IT

Preheat the oven to 170°c fan. Put all the dry ingredients into a large mixing bowl. Melt the vegan butter in a small pan over a low heat. Ensure it is only just melted and don't let it bubble.

Add the melted vegan butter and the coconut or date nectar to the dry mix slowly and carefully, using a wooden spoon to mix and bind everything together until all the ingredients are evenly incorporated and the mix is soft and malleable, not too dry. I do try to make mine crispy and crumbly with as little fat as possible, but if at this stage it seems too dry then do add a little olive oil or a little more melted vegan butter.

Press the flapjack mixture into a baking tray and bake at 170°c fan in the preheated oven until the top is slightly golden. This will take approximately 20 minutes.

When the flapjack is done, cut into squares immediately and then leave to cool in the tray before removing and storing in an airtight container. They are so good that my mouth is watering as I write this!

STEP

12

START
TO GO
WITH
THE FLOW

In psychology, there are four stages of competence or learning involved in gaining a new skill, and you are about to enter into the last stage.

Before something triggered you to take control of what you eat, you were what is known as 'unconsciously incompetent'. In other words, you didn't know what you didn't know. The reason you bought this book was – presumably – you became aware that what you were doing wasn't quite right; you became 'consciously incompetent'. And as you've been working through the changes and making progress, you have become 'consciously competent' at creating healthier, more nutrient-dense foods and ensuring that your home is a haven for 'forward' foods.

Now you're entering the final phase: 'unconscious competence'. This is when things start slotting into place, getting much easier, and happening simply as a matter of course.

WHAT WILL ACTUALLY BE HAPPENING FOR YOU?

In practical terms, you will be getting more and more confident with what you are preparing, cooking, and the way you are managing your and your family's eating habits. Hopefully you'll be starting to relax a bit. At this point, I find that clients are able to move from planning and prepping absolutely everything for the week ahead to having a little less structure and even improvising meals some nights.

After all, when you know that your kitchen only contains good stuff, you can't really go wrong. When you have lists of healthier quick meals at your fingertips, you simply cannot revert to junk.

You will move from batch cooking in your free time to preparing meals on the hoof as well

You will become used to having back-up 'rush night' meals at the ready

You will have batch-cooked food ready in the freezer

You will have your rice, potatoes, and veggies ready and waiting in advance

You will be more flexible in using new foods and introducing new flavours and varieties

You will be enjoying and continually expanding a wider repertoire of meals

You will be getting faster at cooking and prepping so you can become more spontaneous

Above all, you can be confident that you and your family are getting the best possible nourishment for a long and healthy life!

BANOFFEE TART

As far as nutrition goes, this is a clear winner. It also beats boiling a tin for hours to make toffee, which I would walk away and forget about on more than one occasion! It's totally mouth-watering and delicious; my daughter has this in place of a birthday cake and insists on having it for breakfast, lunch and dinner. I used a very large flan dish so adjust the quantities if you want to make a smaller tart.

Preparation time: 30 minutes, plus chilling | Serves: 8-10

WHAT I USE

300g mixed nuts (you could use just almonds if you prefer)
50g coconut chips
4 organic oat biscuits or 60g oats
30 Medjool dates, pitted (approximately, usually about a packet)
30g vegan butter (I use Naturli)
8-9 bananas (depending on size)
2 large tablespoons almond butter (see recipe on page 68)
Dash of coconut water
3 small tins of coconut milk, refrigerated for at least 2 hours
2 large tablespoons unrefined icing sugar
1 vanilla pod (optional)
Sprinkle of rock salt (optional)
Cacao nibs, cacao powder or grated dark chocolate (optional)

HOW I MAKE IT

Throw the nuts, coconut chips and oat biscuits or oats in a food processor and whizz for about a minute until crumbly and consistent in texture. Add ten pitted dates and whizz again.

In a small pan, melt the vegan butter carefully then pour it straight into the processor. Blitz until you have a soft but firm paste that has evenly incorporated all your ingredients. Transfer this to a 30cm flan dish and press down well. There's no need to line it, but you could cover the base with greaseproof paper if you choose. Transfer to the fridge.

The processor bowl should have cleaned itself as the mixture binds, so you can add the remaining 20 dates and four large peeled bananas straight to it, along with the nut butter. Whizz until you have a smooth toffee-like consistency, and add the coconut water if the mixture seems too stiff or thick.

Take the tart base out of the fridge and chop the remaining four or five bananas into roughly 1cm slices. Layer them into the base until it's covered, then carefully pour the toffee filling over them evenly, scraping every last bit from the bowl. Transfer the tart back to the fridge to set.

Take your tins of coconut milk from the fridge and scrape off the solidified cream at the top into a bowl. Save the runnier liquid underneath for your morning smoothie or iced coffee. Beat the coconut cream with a fork for just 30 seconds with the sieved icing sugar (you may want a little more to taste) and, if you like, the seeds from a vanilla pod for extra deliciousness.

Spoon the cream over your toffee layer when it has set, then add a sprinkling of rock salt, cacao nibs, cacao powder or grated dark chocolate if you like. Pop the banoffee tart back in the fridge to chill for at least 1 hour before you serve it.

I change and play around with this recipe each time I make it, and you can too! Sometimes I will add a handful of unsweetened dried banana chips to my base for an extra crunch with the nuts. As an alternative topping, The Coconut Collaborative Chocolate Pots make a great whipped cream. You could also add their banana pots to the toffee layer or topping.

ONE SIZE FITS ALL CAKE

Thinking plant-based cakes must be yuk? I know I used to, but that was before I had a play around with some wonderful, nutritionally dense ingredients to get the combinations just right for this all-purpose, plant-based, scrummy and easily adaptable cake recipe. When I first made this for my son's birthday, I found that it was every bit as delicious as the 46+ cakes I've made for my children's birthdays over the years.

Preparation time: 10 minutes | Cooking time: 30-35 minutes | Serves: 8

WHAT I USE

150g vegan butter, plus extra for greasing (I use Naturli Vegan Block)

300ml organic soy or oat milk

1 tablespoon apple cider vinegar

1 vanilla pod or 1 teaspoon vanilla paste

250g spelt flour, plus extra for dusting

200g organic coconut sugar

50g ground almonds

2 heaped teaspoons baking powder (I used gluten-free)

½ teaspoon bicarbonate of soda

½ teaspoon xanthan gum

For the filling

150g-200g vegan butter (I use Naturli Vegan Block)

2 large oranges, zested

Raw unrefined icing sugar (not the white stuff!)

HOW I MAKE IT

Preheat the oven to 180°c or 160°c fan. Line the bases of two 20cm sandwich tins with baking parchment and grease with a little of the vegan butter. You can of course use dairy butter instead of a plant-based alternative throughout the recipe.

Put the dairy-free milk into a jug and add the vinegar, then leave for a few minutes until it looks a little lumpy.

Split the vanilla pod in half lengthways then scrape half the seeds, or half the paste, into a large bowl with all the other cake ingredients. Pour over the milk mixture and, using an electric whisk or by hand, beat everything together until smooth.

Divide the cake mixture between your two prepared tins then bake them in the centre of the preheated oven for 30 to 35 minutes or until a skewer inserted into the middle of the cakes comes out clean. Leave them in their tins until cool enough to handle then carefully turn out onto wire racks to cool completely. Meanwhile, make the filling.

To make the vegan buttercream, put the butter into a clean bowl with all the orange zest and the remaining vanilla paste or seeds. How much butter you use depends on how much icing you'd like to make. I haven't given you an amount for the icing sugar because it's best to add it little by little through a sieve. Beat or whisk everything together and keep tasting. Add as little sugar as you can so that you are happy with your butter icing without it being overly sweet.

When the cakes are cool, spread the filling on the flattest half, then sandwich them together. Dust the top with unrefined icing sugar if you like.

I served this heaped with dairy-free passion fruit yoghurt (from The Coconut Collaborative) and it is to die for, except with ingredients this good it's actually stuff to live longer for!

BUTTERNUT SQUASH MUFFINS

I make cakes every now and then to say to my teens: "Hey, I know I'm a health freak and sorry for sneaking broccoli and kale into the morning smoothie, but we can still eat cake and indulge too…" Yes, they are full of butternut squash but I promise you, you wouldn't know! Xanthan gum is necessary for wheat-free cooking as it helps to bind the ingredients, and inulin is a dietary fibre. Both are available at good health food shops.

Preparation time: 10 minutes | Cooking time: 15-20 minutes | Makes 15-20

WHAT I USE

400g butternut squash

325g organic coconut sugar

4 large free-range organic eggs or replacements (see below)

150g organic spelt flour

50g organic rice flour

100g organic ground almonds

3 heaped teaspoons baking powder

1 teaspoon ground cinnamon

½ teaspoon xanthan gum

25g inulin (optional)

175ml extra-virgin olive oil

To replace the egg

½ tablespoon ground chia seeds

1 tablespoon ground flax seeds

6 tablespoons almond milk

½ a banana, mashed

½ tablespoon vegan yoghurt

For the topping

1 small tub of cream cheese, mascarpone or vegan alternative

2 tablespoons date or coconut nectar

1 vanilla pod or a few drops of vanilla essence

or

100g butter or vegan alternative (I use Naturli Vegan Block)

3 tablespoons raw cane icing sugar

1 vanilla pod or a few drops of vanilla essence

HOW I MAKE IT

Preheat the oven to 180°c and line a muffin tin with cases. Roughly chop the butternut squash (you can leave the skin on but I don't usually) then whizz the squash in a food processor for a couple of minutes until finely chopped, but not puréed. Next, add the sugar and blend briefly.

If you are using the egg replacement, mix the ground chia and flax seeds with the almond milk. Stir well while it thickens then add to the processor or bowl along with the banana and yoghurt. If you are using the eggs, add them to the butternut and beat to combine.

Slowly mix in the flours, ground almonds, baking powder, cinnamon, xanthan gum and inulin (if using). Combine well but don't mix the batter for any longer than necessary, particularly if you're using an electric food processor. It will add too much air and the muffins will flop. Finally, add the olive oil and whizz to combine once more. You can do all this by hand too.

Divide the batter between the muffin cases and put the tin into the preheated oven. Bake for 15 to 20 minutes, checking that the tops spring back when pressed before taking them out.

While the muffins are baking, choose one of the toppings. If you are using vanilla pods, split them open down the length then scrape along each half of the pod to take out the seeds, which are the part you want here. Simply combine all the ingredients for either the cream cheese icing or the buttercream and beat together until smooth or light and fluffy. Apply liberally to the muffins when they have cooled. Decorate with walnuts and fresh or dried fruit if you like.

A note on the flours: I always use mixed flours for a blend of nutrients, and I love to add the almonds for texture, protein and vitamins. But if you don't have more than one flour to hand, or any nuts, then this works just as well with one flour.

WHAT'S NEXT?

You've done it! You've transformed your eating habits as well as those of your household. So what happens now?

HOW CAN YOU KEEP ON TRACK?

Keep asking questions, exploring, and looking for ways to upgrade the way you and your family are eating.

Seek out new ways to 'upgrade' what you are eating and set yourself new challenges.

Keep checking labels and building your understanding around the food you are choosing and eating.

Join a foodie Facebook group for inspiration and support! It goes without saying that you'd be welcome in mine.

Get in the habit of reading books that will expand and update your knowledge around food and health. This will start to change and inform your thinking, which gives you much more chance of sustaining the changes you are making.

You might even want to sign up for healthy food and nutrition summits. There are many to choose from every year and they often feature pioneers in healthy eating, such as Dr Mark Hyman and Dr Michael Greger and Ocean Robbins (of the Baskin Robbins ice cream empire fame, whose parents swapped this inheritance for a plant-based diet on the beach. In fact, they nearly named him Kale!).

REFLECTION

Now is also a perfect opportunity to go back through your diary and look at the most significant things you have learned each week. Write them down somewhere separately.

Then go back through your diary and find the two or three 'wins' that you noted at the start of each week. Write these down too.

These two lists – your 'lessons learned' and 'achievements' – both represent an important shift in who you are and your approach to your life, and they are proof that you really can make your goals a reality. You will also have undergone a huge change in your self-awareness and personal development and these lists can serve as a reminder of that.

You can decide what you want to do with them; perhaps keep them in your wallet as a constant reminder of your ability to move forward, pop them on the fridge, or save a picture of them on your phone. Now you have gone through this disciplined process of change, you know you can do it again and have valuable skills that are transferable to other areas of your life.

CHAPTER 4

TOOLBOX

I never wanted to just write a recipe book. I wanted to spur parents into action, to help them feel empowered and understood, and to do this, I needed to write a book that was accessible and inspiring. This section of the book is crucial in achieving this aim. It pulls together a whole range of tips and tricks that will help you at any point along your 12-step journey.

HOW TO READ FOOD LABELS

If you are to take just one thing from this book, then let it be label reading, as it will raise your level of awareness hugely in terms of the foods you buy. I would also advise looking at ingredients labels rather than nutrition labels, or at least in this order. It will help you get a clear idea of what is in the food you're buying and in what quantity, and then you can delve deeper into the detail if you need to.

INGREDIENTS

Ingredients are listed in order of predominance, with the ingredients used in the largest quantity appearing first in the list. You'll likely find that some products are called something entirely misleading and that the 'named' ingredient makes up only a tiny part of the product. Often, this will be the most expensive ingredient. For example, I once bought a beetroot spelt organic sourdough loaf as part of an online shop, and when it arrived, I found that the beetroot comprised only 3%. The spelt was also diluted with wheat flour.

NUTRITION LABELS

1. Energy

The terms 'kJ' and 'kcal' (calories) tell you how much energy is in a product. Women need an average of 2,000 kcal a day and men need 2,500 kcal on average.

2. Saturates

Saturates is another word for saturated fat. This tells you about the amount of saturated fat in the product.

3. Salt

Most adults eat more salt than the recommended maximum of 6g a day, increasing their risk of high blood pressure. You may see 'sodium' listed rather than salt. To convert sodium into salt, multiply the amount on the label by 2.5.

4. Reference intake (RI)

Formerly known as the recommended daily amount (RDA), reference intakes are useful guidelines on the amount of energy and nutrients you need for a healthy balanced diet each day. In essence, this is the daily dietary intake level of a nutrient considered sufficient by the Food and Nutrition Board of the Institute of Medicine to meet the requirements of healthy adults. The %RI tells you how much of your daily healthy maximum is in the portion of the product.

The %RI for an adult is based on the following values:

kcal	Fat	Saturates	Sugars	Salt
2000	70g	20g	90g	6g

5. Serving/portion size

The portion size on the pack is the manufacturer's recommendation for one portion of the product. The %RI is worked out based on this portion size. Some packs also show the amount of each nutrient in 100g of the product. This will be given in grams or millilitres.

A manufacturer's idea of a portion size might be smaller than yours, which means that even if a product looks healthy, if you have more than this portion amount, you may end up consuming more calories, saturated fat or salt than you realise.

HOW TO STOCK YOUR CUPBOARDS

This section is all about getting the right stuff in, throwing the wrong stuff out, setting your environment up for success, sorting out your substitutes, and experimenting with 'flavour foods' so you can make totally delicious food.

There is no way that I could tell you exactly how to stock your cupboards, and nor would I want to, since you may well end up buying a whole set of foods that you then never use. I can, however, give you some guidelines to help you start thinking about what sorts of things you might want to stock in your fridge and cupboards and hopefully help you discover other things that will become a vital ingredient for you. I can also give you hints and tips on everyday items that I use to transform food from bland to tasty in a matter of seconds, and that enhance nutrition in the process.

I recommend starting by introducing one or two new foods or ingredients into your recipes or weekly shop, such as one new pulse or type of flour. This, along with gradually eliminating the 'empty calorie' versions you are replacing, will be a huge step forward. Good substitutes add up to sustainable, long-term change.

Before we get into the details, it's also worth mentioning that I choose organic ingredients whenever possible. I believe this offers myself and my family the purest foods that are free from pesticides, herbicides and insecticides and therefore better for us. This isn't always possible due to availability or budget but, generally, it is a rule I work to.

FRESH FOODS

As mentioned in Step 1, your weekly shopping should be split roughly 50:50, so that fresh food forms half of your shop and everything else the other half.

I am not going to list every vegetable you could buy here, of course, but make sure that you are including a mix of cruciferous vegetables (such as cauliflower, cabbage, kale), root vegetables, dark green leafy vegetables, stoned fruits (including avocado*), celery and alliums (onions, garlic, leeks and shallots). Fresh ginger is also a staple in my house, along with fresh turmeric. Similarly, with fruits, make sure you buy a mix. Include berries, citrus fruits (lemons are great to have around for both drinks and cooking), stoned fruits, tropical fruits (such as bananas and mangos) and apples.

*Avocados are one of very few 'complete foods', containing all the nourishment we need. They are rich in monounsaturated fats, potassium, B-vitamins, and folic acid. When combined with other foods, avocados also act as a nutrient booster to help the body to absorb cancer-fighting nutrients such as carotenoids (including spinach and carrots).

TINS

As long as you use them alongside a range of fresh ingredients, tins can be a wonderful way to have the right stuff ready when you need it to add into the food you are making.

I don't mean tins of prepared soups, sauces, baked beans, and pastas, but chickpeas, mixed beans, black beans, cannellini, pinto, kidney and borlotti beans, chopped tomatoes, lentils, and more. I usually buy about 14 tins a week. This may seem like a huge amount, but I have a few staple recipes that deplete these in a matter of days.

Try starting with one of each and see if you can incorporate them into your weekly meals. Tinned tomatoes are a good one to start with. Try adding them to soups, Bolognese sauces, pasta dishes, casseroles or curries.

It's still important to check all labels before buying tins of anything to ensure there are no additives, flavourings, or hidden sugars or salts. You will also want to check the tins themselves; many of them will be lined with BPA, which is found in the lining of most aluminium cans and can be toxic. Trusted brands I use for tins include Biona and Mr Organic. Similarly, be aware that many tea bags contain plastics such as polypropylene to seal them, which is not biodegradable, recyclable or beneficial to our health. Brands I recommend here are Abel and Cole, Clipper, Pukka, Tea Pigs, Co-op own brand, Twinings pyramid range, Waitrose Duchy range and Dragonfly main organic range.

CONDIMENTS, FLAVOURINGS AND STOCK

Having a supply of herbs, spices, condiments, and stock on hand will help you make more flavoursome meals.

Stock up on herbs and spices. I buy fresh basil and coriander every week and get through masses of each, but I still have a cupboard packed with dried herbs, spices, powders and seeds for curries (cumin, fennel, fenugreek, garam masala), lime leaves, mustard powder, Chinese five spice, nigella seeds, and fresh chillies. If you are starting from scratch, some paprika, some mixed herbs, and a good curry powder would be a starting point. It's also very easy to grow herbs such as rosemary and mint, which I have in the garden, or even counter-top chillies.

Get yourself a really good stock that you can use to bolster recipes. If you have the time, homemade stock can be worth the effort, but I love Marigold Bouillon Powder. Not only is it delicious, but it doesn't contain yeast. Most stock cubes include lots of this, and we simply do not need it. Check labels and find one you are happy with.

Use healthier oils for dressings and cooking. I would advise a choice of extra-virgin olive oil, rapeseed oil, avocado and nut oils. I personally love sesame seed oil in my dressings, but experiment and see which you prefer.

Buy raw apple cider vinegar with the mother, which is great in dressings, sauces and marinades (see page 177 as to why we should be having this daily).

Try miso. Made from fermented soy beans, miso is protein-rich and good for the digestive system. You can usually buy a white or brown version. I keep mine in the fridge and add it to soups, sauces, and a huge range of other foods.

Minimise all sweeteners and eliminate the white, processed stuff. For healthier options, try organic jaggery, date nectar or dates, coconut nectar, manuka honey or coconut sugar.

Buy organic black pepper and a good salt, preferably rock, sea, or Himalayan.

Try nutritional yeast. A good source of B12, nutritional yeast is delicious as a topping for so many foods including crispy potatoes, wedges and crispy chickpeas.

Consider other flavour staples, such as lemon juice, lime juice, tamari (a wheat-free version of soy sauce), Worcestershire sauce (vegan or otherwise), Tabasco, jalapeños, gherkins or pickles.

RICE, PASTA, AND THE STORE CUPBOARD

Red Camargue rice

Wild rice

Brown basmati rice

Brown short grain rice

Vegetable pastas/lentil pastas

Spelt/wholemeal pastas

Quinoa (I prefer mixed grains)

Bulgar wheat

Wholegrain couscous

Large wholegrain couscous

FLOURS

Spelt

Rye

Buckwheat

Cornflour

Coconut

Wholewheat

BAKING

Coconut

Coconut flakes

Creamed coconut

Coconut cream (different from the above, usually tinned)

Coconut flour

Coconut sugar

Coconut nectar

Coconut oil

Oats

Seeds

Wheat-free baking powder

Bicarbonate of soda

Xanthan gum

Dried banana

Dried fruits

Cinnamon

Vanilla (pod, powder, or essence)

Almond essence

Cacao nibs

Carob

PULSES

If you have the time to buy dried beans and pulses, do so. Ensure they are washed and soaked well and cook as directed (I choose to buy tins instead, apart from red lentils which I can use without pre-soaking, because I find they are less gassy when digested).

Red lentils

Split peas

Puy lentils

Black beans

Borlotti beans

Cannellini beans

Kidney beans

Pinto beans

OTHER POWDERS, NUTS AND SEEDS

Cacao powder

Chia seeds

Nuts: A great source of protein. Buy flaked, whole, mixed, and varieties of many so that you can snack on them as well as use them in cooking and baking.

Pine nuts

Pumpkin seeds

Sunflower seeds

Poppy seeds

Linseeds

Maca

Chlorella

BICARBONATE OF SODA

Why am I including this mundane everyday ingredient? Because it is a super ingredient with powers beyond its humble status in the kitchen. It can be used in a myriad of ways from cleaning to teeth whitening, from insect bites to heartburn and maybe even as an agent against cancer by stabilising natural healing dynamics.

FROZEN FOODS

I often get asked if frozen foods are as good for us as fresh. When it comes to fruit and vegetables, the answer is yes. They are frozen so soon after the point of picking or harvesting that the nutrients are retained. My preference for taste and sometimes texture is usually fresh, but it is useful to have back-up options in the freezer for those nights you might run out of your usual vegetables and fruits. Frozen fruit and veg also works particularly well in smoothies (a good way to pack in at least three portions of your ten a day) and ice lollies (see pages 134 and 136).

DRINKS

Apart from water, which you should be topping up on constantly, ensure you have a good stock of the following:

Teas and infusions

Coconut water

Pressed juices/freshly squeezed juices. Ensure you choose those with the pulp included for extra fibre. I dilute them with 50% water.

Coffee (in moderation)

Fresh ginger, lemon, and turmeric in hot water (for an immune-boosting tonic every morning)

Drinking orange juice is a common choice for mornings, but beware of too much fructose early on in the day. On an empty stomach, it may not do your gut and liver any good. It can also be acidic and while it does contain valuable vitamin C, the combination of sugar (most shop-bought orange juice is very high in sugars) and acid early in the day might cause indigestion.

MILKS

Even if dairy still forms part of your diet, an easy way to cut down is by swapping to an alternative milk, such as:

Oat

Coconut

Almond

Hazelnut

Rice

Soya (if you buy sweetened, ensure this has been done with apple juice or similar)

My top tip here is to mix the milks. Some are much thinner than others, and if you are used to dairy, you may find this unpalatable. Soya is thicker and combines well with others. I do use soya exclusively for my white sauces, as it works perfectly for them and does not have a strong taste.

If you are thinking of swapping to dairy-free milk, don't expect your tea or coffee to taste the same; it won't. Again, this is about finding an alternative. I landed on white tea: a more refined version of green tea (which I find bitter) but with all the same antioxidant properties. I prefer Dragonfly White Tea which is both smooth and refreshing.

CHEESES

Cheese is harder to advise on since I have been dairy-free for a long time. As a rule, goat and sheep products – while still classed as dairy – will be more digestible. They are not as mass produced as many products made from cow's milk. But, overall, my advice is to try to cut down on cheese. We can get the calcium it provides from our vegetables and elsewhere and protein from pulses, nuts, tofu, tempeh, edamame, green peas and more. It really does not do us much good. That said, vegan cheeses are improving in quality. My personal preference is Violife.

WHAT TO COOK WITH

There is a lot of research showing that utensils and non-stick aluminium pans can lead to aluminium seeping into food, so consider replacing these with stainless steel, ceramic, and cast-iron options. This isn't necessarily something you'll be able to do straight away, but I have slowly grown my selection of baking trays, frying pans, and saucepans.

As part of setting yourself up for success, it's also worth investing in a few other kitchen items to make life a bit easier for you. In order of importance for me, these would be:

A GOOD SET OF KNIVES

You are more likely to cut yourself on a blunt knife. Not only this, but it is frustrating and hard to use blunt knives. They don't need to be expensive, but perhaps invest in a good sharpener.

A NUTRIBULLET OR ANY GOOD BLENDER

Given that I use this at least twice a day to make a minimum of seven smoothies, milkshakes, and other drinks, this was one of the best investments I have made in the kitchen. It enables me to send the children off with at least three pieces of fruit and veg in them before they've walked out the door and ensures a smooth consistency which you will need to avoid any resistance. I also use it to make ice lollies, sauces, and toppings.

FOOD PROCESSOR

You will inevitably get some crossover with your blender here, but again, my processor is in constant use. I am actually on to my third in 14 years just because, while it is one of the best on the market and I would not be without it, I have simply worn it out. Do your research and see what is best for you but do invest in one that will stand the test of time and be robust enough for family use. Use it for a myriad of foods, from cakes and biscuits to falafel, burgers of any sort, nut roast, creamy mash, salsa, and so much more.

MY STEAMER

I steam nearly everything in my stainless steel steamer. It ensures you don't overcook vegetables and you can still use the water as stock, so you don't throw any of those lovely nutrients away.

HAND BLENDER

Great for soups and very cheap to buy.

UTENSILS

As you progress on your journey, there's no doubt you'll find that you are missing other tools in the kitchen that enable you to produce the food you want to. Not necessarily anything complicated or expensive, but simple things like a sieve or two to wash your vegetables, graters, a large bowl or two, serving spoons, a measuring jug, and even a good tin opener. I'd add my slotted spoon, large serving spoon and a wooden set of utensils to this list including some sort of rolling pin and wooden cooking fork which I use for things like Bolognese, chilli and most meals I make on the hob.

TEENAGERS:
A SPECIAL
MENTION

As a mum and as a food coach, I have begun to focus on support for teenagers as a category in its own right. Though they're effectively still children, adolescents face such huge change and stresses in these years, not least preparing for life away from their parents. And rarely does a week go by without mention of childhood obesity and the long-term health risks this poses, such as Type 2 diabetes.

For us as parents, when our children become teenagers, we start to lose control, and not just over what they eat: they are out more than they are home, in their room more than in communal areas, on their phone more than talking to us, and with their friends more than they are with family. So what can we do to help? Food isn't everything, but it's a much bigger part of the equation than you might think.

It's normal for teenagers to experiment with their growing independence and to try new things, maybe even rebelling against what has always been the norm in the family home. And in spending more time out and with friends, they adopt pack-like practices of eating at similar places and eating similar things. Standing out from the crowd is not something most teenagers aspire to. Unfortunately, being 'healthy' is not seen as cool for a reason I am not sure I understand but definitely have to accept. Instead, it seems to be about what looks cool, which I am guessing broccoli and chickpeas do not!

Added to stresses relating to friends and fitting in is – of course – peer pressure. But I would venture to say that, in the UK at least, school and exams are the primary source of worry for teenagers.

Then, of course, there's appearance. The likes of Snapchat and Instagram mean that many teens are almost constantly taking photos of themselves and posting on one platform or another. As a result, they are hyper aware of their looks and how other people will judge them. It is no surprise, really, that teenage eating disorders are so prevalent.

So what can we do to support our teenagers as they go through this turbulent time? As parents, we can't alleviate their anxieties or stresses altogether, but there is an awful lot we can do with food to exact a chemical change and enable their bodies and minds to deal with different situations. And of course, we need to instil the right values when it comes to looks and acceptance, but we also need to teach those all-important lessons around food, ingredients, and health. So often these are misunderstood by teenagers who choose to eat very little of the wrong stuff, when platefuls of the right stuff will maintain a level weight and nourish their bodies and minds.

First, we need to understand that – as with all of us – there are three foundations underpinning teenager's health: nutrition, sleep, and exercise: the 'Triangle of Health'. Above anything else, as parents we should be actively supporting each of these elements in the best way we can to ensure our teens are happy, healthy and safe, which for me are the only things that matter.

NUTRITION

Prioritise good nutrition. It has the biggest singular impact on the health and wellbeing of your teens. Make it as easy as possible for your teens by stocking your cupboards with healthy snacks (see page 146), nourishing up favourite dishes (see page 100), and swapping out nasties for nutritious alternatives (see page 50).

Encourage a plant-based diet. There is a growing body of evidence that a plant-based diet is our best option in terms of proactive health insurance. While they may never want to go fully plant-based, try to get them on the spectrum and educate them about the wealth of scientific evidence out there.

Help them recognise and understand the foods that do them damage: bacon, processed meats, red meats, sugar, dairy etc.

SLEEP

Make sure they get enough sleep. Recent research, particularly Why We Sleep by Matthew Walker, is – ironically – a huge wake up call. If we don't get enough sleep, our bodies suffer considerably. It affects mental acuity, the ageing process, and can be a contributory factor to chronic disease.

Set sleep alarms on their phones or watches so they know when to be in bed for optimal sleep, dictated by the time they have to be up. Sleeping for long enough, at the right time, gives the body time to regenerate, restore, and function optimally which will support both mental and physical health. It also supports good gut health which is the basis of our immunity, and works in synergy with the circadian rhythms where there is an intersection with metabolism.

Keep phones out of the bedroom if possible so the first and last thing they do cannot be checking their phone. It also means they can't be tempted to look at a text that arrives at 2am after which they will not be able to get back to sleep.

EXERCISE

Promote exercise. Teenagers are under a lot of pressure, and exercise is an important way to manage this by releasing endorphins. Have you ever seen them come back low after a football match, swimming, hockey, cricket or dancing? Encourage them to continue with any active interest picked up in school. In fact, we should all be aiming to do some form of exercise every day, and a variety: cardiovascular, strength, weight bearing and endurance.

Encourage them to include a meditative aspect, as in yoga or tai chi.

HOW TO SUPPORT TEENAGE ANXIETY AND DEPRESSION THROUGH FOOD

The epidemic concerning our teens and mental health warrants a look at what we can do with food to alleviate some of the issues, things we can do as parents apart from support with constant love and simply 'being there'.

Avoid caffeine and cut down on sugar. Both can give us a crazy high and then dump us very low. They can also affect bowel movements which in turn can make us feel down.

Increase fruits and veggies.

Eat more grains and seeds and cut out the sugar-loaded biscuits, cakes and junk. Smart complex carbohydrates will stop the craving for sugars and bad carbs and help boost mood in the process.

Get the protein in.

Only let the good fats in!

Build the gut biome and healthy bacteria. There is increasing evidence that our gut microbiome is our second brain. Not only does it build immunity, but a healthy gut has influence over the way we are feeling and our mood, manufacturing over 90% of our serotonin.

Try a Mediterranean diet: lots of fish, olives, olive oil, legumes and salads.

Prioritise foods like spinach, seeds, nuts and soya products, on a plant-based diet, or turkey, tuna and chicken which contain an amino acid called tryptophan. Tryptophan is thought to help make serotonin and play a role in healthy sleep: both crucial for teens!

Consider supplements but speak to a specialist about this. The likelihood of depression is higher in people with low Vitamin D, for example.

Eat foods rich in selenium. Often cited as 'anti-cancer', selenium has now also been shown to ward off low mood. It is possible to have too much, though, so stick to foods not supplements. The best way is two Brazil nuts a day! How easy is that?

PACKED LUNCHES FOR TEENS

School is such a huge part of teenagers' lives – in terms of exams, friendships, peer pressure – so sending them off with a good packed lunch every day is one of the best ways to support them. Step 8 in Chapter 3 gives you detailed guidance about what comprises a good lunch, but you should also make sure that lunches for teens:

Prioritise long-lasting, slow-releasing energy from complex carbohydrates: no empty calorie foods as a quick fix

Feed all-important friendly bacteria and support digestion

Are made up of at least 50% fibre in the form of fruit and vegetables

Taste great!

Don't stand out too much from the crowd if your teen is self conscious (although my daughter's definitely did, and after a number of comments initially, most days her friends became very envious of what she took for lunch every day)

WHAT ELSE CAN WE DO?

Maximise the minimised time you have with your teenager by focusing on what is most important to them. In general, these are some of the most important factors in a teenager's life:

Their skin

Their looks and clothing

Overall image

Self esteem

Energy levels

Brain function

Digestion

Mood

Balancing hormones

Relationships/friendships

It's worth being aware of these major trigger points for our teenagers in order to be able to best support them nutritionally and overall with their wellbeing. This goes beyond what you feed them when they are at home. It's about how you educate them, too, the messages you send and how you connect with them. It has to resonate to make the slightest difference. It can be a difficult line to tread to avoid seeming overbearing, and be mindful that they will want to exert their own opinions on things now too. As a mum of three, I understand just how challenging this time can be and it is very much a balance.

CHAPTER 5

TERM
BUSTING
A-Z

DEMYSTIFYING THE WORDS USED AROUND FOOD

The language and terms used to describe food can be overwhelming, but we are only able to make sustainable changes in terms of our relationship with food if we can understand it.

As a consumer, it is hard to make the right choices for you and your family through this maze of 'food language'. Even deciphering the way in which foods are labelled can be challenging. To help make things a little clearer, I've created a glossary to demystify some of the terms we hear bandied about regularly.

Of course, this is by no means an exhaustive list. That would be another book entirely and there are other experts much better placed to do that than me. What you find here is a mum who started from scratch on her own food journey, educating herself along the way, sharing some of the things she has learnt. They are areas of priority as I see them, and I hope you will find them useful. Some of them may seem very simple and familiar, but I have included them nonetheless as they have an important bearing on health.

A2 COW'S MILK

Most milks contain A1 and A2 proteins, which some find hard to digest. A2 cow's milk contains only A2 protein, making it easier to digest. This milk has been called the 'original milk' since it is only due to the domestication of farm cattle that cow's milk now contains both.

ALKALINE FOODS

Foods that have an alkalising effect on the body when we eat or drink them. It is a point of contention that alkalinity can offer health benefits for the body but the general argument is that an alkaline body may offer more protection, whereas acidity may make us more vulnerable to disease.

ANTIBACTERIAL

Sometimes called natural antibiotics, antibacterial foods fight the 'bad' bacteria. They can be used as a home remedy to treat minor illnesses, even flu. The most antibacterial foods include:

Garlic

Echinacea

Manuka honey

Ginger

Goldenseal

Oregano

Grapefruit seed extract

Apple cider vinegar

Horseradish

Onions

Cinnamon

Turmeric

ANTIFUNGAL

Foods that have an antifungal effect on the body. Many of us suffer from a condition called candida, a fungal infection or overgrowth that we are likely unaware of. Candida plays havoc with our digestion and can cause a whole host of other symptoms, including thrush in women. It is caused by an overgrowth of yeast in the gut (which is why I constantly advise checking labels for this addition) and can be combatted by healthy bacteria and antifungal foods. It will be fed by sugars, antibiotics, hidden and overt yeasts in products, alcohol, grains and high-sugar fruits. Antifungal foods include prebiotics, coconut oil, and curcumin found in turmeric (see also yeast).

ANTI-INFLAMMATORY

In the context of food, an anti-inflammatory is an ingredient that will reduce the inflammation in our bodies or help to keep it at bay. With inflammation widely accepted as the major cause of chronic and acute health conditions, anti-inflammatory foods should be a major part of our diets.

Many brightly coloured fresh foods contain anti-inflammatory carotenoids and flavonoids, so remember to always choose foods that have the strongest colour if possible, for example, red cabbage or onions as opposed to white. Other top anti-inflammatory foods include:

Turmeric (a real superfood if ever there was one!)

Green leafy vegetables (spinach and kale)

Blueberries (since they contain quercetin which is a powerful antioxidant)

Strawberries

Oranges

Cherries

Pineapples

Wild (as opposed to farmed) salmon

Flax seeds

Chia seeds

Tomatoes

Nuts

Broccoli

Avocado

Peppers

ANTIOXIDANTS

Found in many fruits and vegetables, antioxidants protect you from free radicals, which are believed to contribute to the ageing process and play a part in major diseases (see also free radicals).

ANTIVIRAL

Foods and herbs that may help to fight viruses in the body and naturally boost the immune system. They include:

Oregano

Garlic

Echinacea

Olive leaf

Ginger

Liquorice root

Elderberry

Shiitake mushrooms (these also have antibacterial and antifungal properties)

Apple cider vinegar

Cinnamon

APPLE CIDER VINEGAR

A wonderful vinegar if unrefined and unpasteurised, with many health benefits from boosting immunity and long-term health to alleviating colds and sore throats and helping with more serious health concerns such as diabetes, cancer, heart problems, and high cholesterol. Antiviral and antibiotic, apple cider vinegar is wonderful for the stomach, if you always buy a brand containing the 'mother' (a colony of beneficial live bacteria). You will see this as a cloudy sediment at the bottom of the bottle. It can also aid digestion and help with tummy bugs. I take 15 millilitres a day, but you can also add it to dressings, soups, and sauces.

BMI (BODY MASS INDEX)

A measurement intended to identify whether a person is of a healthy weight. It is obtained by dividing your weight in kilograms by the square of your height in metres. It can be deceptive and not always a reliable way to gauge your correct weight, because it makes no account for muscle mass, bone density and overall body composition in addition to racial and sex differences.

CAFFEINE

An addictive chemical found in coffee, cacao, tea, coke or cola, and many other products. People often use it to maintain mental alertness because it is a central nervous stimulant. Caffeine blocks the effect of adenosine in the brain preventing fatigue and increasing arousal, alertness, and focus. This can have a negative effect on sleep and can lead to anxiety and restlessness. Too much caffeine can also cause headaches and other minor ailments.

Recently, however, caffeine has hit the news for its health benefits. Experts from the University of Southampton and Edinburgh found that people who drink more coffee are less likely to develop a primary form of liver cancer. Harvard researchers showed that drinking four or five cups a day cuts the risk of Parkinson's Disease (2015) and that it may lower your risk of Type 2 diabetes (2014), while the American Cancer Society reports that caffeine may lower your risk of mouth and throat cancer.

CALORIES

In short, a unit of energy. Kilocalories tell us how much energy a certain food will give us. Some foods can be high in calories and calorific value, but contain no nutrients. This is why I urge people to count nutrients, not calories.

CARBOHYDRATE

A macronutrient from sugars, fibres, and starches. Carbohydrates provide the body with glucose, which is then converted to energy. It is found in two forms: complex (healthy) and simple (unhealthy). Complex carbohydrates are minimally processed wholegrains, vegetables, fruit, beans and pulses. They also provide us with phytonutrients, fibre, minerals and vitamins. Unhealthy carbohydrates include highly processed breads, cakes, pastries, fizzy drinks, and refined foods. These foods are easily digested, cause a spike in insulin levels and may lead to weight gain and even diabetes.

CAROTENOIDS

Plant pigments responsible for the bright orange, red, and yellow colours in many fruits and vegetables. They may help provide protective health benefits against chronic disease, notably cancer and eye disease. Examples of foods rich in carotenoids include:

Carrots

Butternut squash

Red and yellow peppers

Tomatoes

CHOLESTEROL

An organic, waxy, fatty substance found in the blood. It is vital to us and is a major component of all cell membranes, used to make fat soluble vitamins, bile to help digestion, and even hormones. Cholesterol is mainly made in our liver, but it is also found in foods. It is carried around your body by proteins of which there are two types: HDL and LDL, high- and low-density lipoproteins.

HDL carries cholesterol away from cells back to the cleansing liver where it is broken down or passed out. LDL, on the other hand, carries cholesterol to the cells. While we do need this, if there is too much, the cholesterol builds up, furring the arteries and raising our risk of heart disease.

CORN-FED

Animals, usually poultry, that have been predominantly fed on corn.

CRUCIFEROUS VEGETABLES

Vegetables that belong to the Brassicaceae family of plants, such as broccoli, brussels sprouts, cauliflower, cabbage, and turnips. Cruciferous vegetables are all low in calories but high in nutrients such as Vitamin A, C, and K, as well as being high in fibre.

Some of the benefits of cruciferous vegetables are their ability to fight cancer compounds, promote oestrogen balance, maintain a healthy heart, reduce inflammation, and regulate blood sugar. If you have a thyroid issue, it is advisable to eat cruciferous vegetables more sparingly and only when cooked.

DAIRY

Products made from mammal milks, such as milk and cheese. Generally, we are more used to using the term to describe products from a cow, however, many people find it easier to digest goat's and sheep's milk. This is because the lactose in these milks changes to lactic acid, and their milks are formed with shorter amino acid protein chains, which are easier on the digestive system.

DIETS

The word diet is associated with losing weight, however, a diet is simply the way that you eat, the foods you consume, and what you drink.

ECHINACEA

A herb often used mostly in winter to support and boost the immune system.

ENERGY (K/CAL)

Used on labels to show us how much energy and calories the food will give us (see also calories).

EPSOM SALTS

A mineral compound of magnesium and sulphate, named after the location of the spring where it was first distilled. Epsom salt looks and feels like any other rock or sea salt, but it has a number of additional properties thanks to its magnesium content. Bathing in water with Epsom salts may relax you, relieve cramping, pain and headaches, improve cardiovascular health and even help to reduce blood sugar. It can be taken orally for other ailments including constipation but consult your doctor or medical practitioner first.

FASTING

A process whereby people give the body and the digestive system a break to empty it and allow DNA to regenerate before eating again. There is a huge body of evidence emerging to support the health benefits of fasting so I would encourage you to read around this yourself. There are also many ways to fast including the 3/2 system or simply eating only a minimal breakfast and waiting until dinner. Many people extend their overnight fast or eat only within a given window of time during the day.

FATS

An essential substance that provides us with energy and helps the body absorb certain vitamins. However, not all fats are created equal. Some fats are good for us and form part of a healthy diet, but others can have a negative impact on our hearts. Saturated fats in particular may play a part in inflammatory diseases.

'Good fats' will generally be more liquid at room temperature. They are said to be 'heart healthy' and monounsaturated or polyunsaturated. Research consistently shows HDL (good cholesterol) is significantly improved by eating nuts, avocados, and good oils. Omega 3s (alpha linolenic acid) found in fatty fish such as salmon, trout, sardines, and herring are particularly good for us, but you can also get these from walnuts, flax seeds, hemp seeds, chia seeds, soya beans and in leafy green vegetables in small amounts if you follow a vegetarian or plant-based diet.

'Bad fats' are generally considered to be trans fats and saturated fats. You should avoid trans fats entirely and keep saturated fats to a minimum. Trans fats are hydrogenated oils, made by changing the molecular make-up of the foods. These fats can raise LDL, the bad form of cholesterol, and inhibit the HDL, the good cholesterol which we need. They can be found in deep-fried fast foods, any sort of margarine and other processed foods. As a rough guide, saturated fats are those that remain hard at room temperature. They are usually animal fats or associated with animals, such as cuts of meat, milk, cheese, butter, lard, ice cream and tropical oils, including coconut oil.

The jury is currently out about the benefits or dangers of coconut oil: it is a saturated fat, but touted as a superfood; some believe it benefits HDL, others that it hinders it. Either way, we should generally use as little extra oil, in any form, as possible.

FAT-FREE, REDUCED-FAT, AND LOW-FAT PRODUCTS

Low fat means a product has less than 3g of fat per 100g, while reduced fat means a product is 25% lower in fat than the standard product. You will often see 'reduced fat' on foods that were very high in fat to start with, for example mayonnaise, crisps, and cheese. You still need to limit how much you eat as the reduced fat version is likely to be high in fat.

Fat-free means that a food contains less than 0.5g of fat per serving. Unfortunately, in my experience, 'fat-free' means 'taste-free', so manufacturers add artificial flavours, salts, sugars, thickeners, flours and additives, resulting in a very unhealthy product with minimum nutrient value.

FIBRE

An essential part of a healthy diet. It keeps our digestive system moving and feeds our gut biome. Fibre can be found in vegetables, fruit, beans, pulses, legumes, and wholefoods. There is strong evidence to show that eating plenty of fibre is associated with lower risks of chronic diseases, including diabetes, strokes, and bowel cancer.

FLAVENOIDS

A diverse group of phytonutrients found in almost all fruit and vegetables, thought to provide antioxidant health benefits.

FLEXITARIAN

A person who eats a primarily vegetarian diet, occasionally including meat and fish.

FREE RADICALS

Toxic by-products of oxygen metabolism that may cause damage to living cells in a process called oxidative stress. Free radicals contain unpaired electrons, meaning that they are volatile and reactive with other structures. They can effectively 'steal' electrons from DNA, proteins, and cell membranes, which cause long-term illness and ageing. Antioxidant foods are thought to help protect us from this, however, this is still an area in which much research needs to be done (see also antioxidant).

FREE-RANGE

A type of breeding whereby the animals are left to roam freely and enjoy a better quality of life, as opposed to battery farming, in which animals are kept in inhumane conditions with limited space and freedom. However, 'free-range' can be used misleadingly, so it's worth doing your research about specific products.

GLUTEN

A family of proteins found in grains such as wheat, rye, spelt, and barley. Gluten contains two main proteins: gliadin and glutenin. Gliadin has a glue-like property, which makes bread elastic and sticky, and is responsible for most of the negative health effects or intolerances you might have heard about when it comes to gluten.

The term coeliac describes people who are allergic to gluten. For them, eating gluten triggers an autoimmune response that attacks the lining of the small intestine. As a result, the body struggles to absorb nutrients in the bloodstream, which can lead to anaemia, then weight loss, and a deterioration in overall health.

Many people these days claim to have gluten sensitivity, indicated by IBS or digestive issues. Though this is an area of some controversy, gluten is now often seen as something to avoid. Despite this bad reputation, though, many can tolerate it well.

GLYCAEMIC INDEX (GI) AND GLYCAEMIC LOAD (GL)

GI is a way to measure how rapidly a food's carbohydrates are digested and released as glucose to raise blood sugar levels. The higher the GI, the more a food will raise your blood sugar. GL, on the other hand, is a ranking system that measures the amount of carbohydrates in a serving of food. A low GL score indicates that a food won't have a bad impact on blood glucose levels.

As GI does not take into account the amount of carbohydrates in a food, GL is often a better indicator of how a particular food will affect blood sugar. Carrots are a great example of this as they have a high GI (71) but a low GL (6). This means that you would have to eat considerable amounts of carrot for it to have much effect on your blood sugar levels.

GM FOODS

Sometimes known as genetically engineered foods, GM (genetically modified) foods have been produced from organisms with DNA that has been changed using genetic engineering.

GRASS-FED

Animals that are fed predominantly on grass, usually used with beef.

GUT FLORA (MICROBIOME)

Living inside our gut are between 300 and 500 kinds of bacteria numbering in the tens of trillions of microorganisms, with more than three million genes. Along with other organisms, fungi, and viruses, these bacteria make up what is called the gut flora, otherwise known as the microbiome or microbiota. The composition of the gut flora is unique to each individual, and is dictated by our diet, our mother and lifestyle. Research now suggests that the glut flora may have the single biggest impact on our wellbeing, mental health, and overall immunity.

HEART-HEALTHY

An adjective used to describe foods that will benefit your cardiovascular system and in particular your heart function. However, this term tends to be used too liberally, so consider with caution.

HIDDEN SUGARS

Sugars that we don't necessarily expect to find in our foods. This includes, for example, sugar that is added to processed or prepared foods as well as naturally occurring sugars in fruits (fructose) and milks (lactose). Take care to examine labels carefully for hidden sugars. Some of the worst culprits include:

Cereal and granola

Soups

Dressings

Sauces

Smoothies

Snack bars

Yoghurts

Bread

Savoury biscuits/crackers

Alcohol

However, sugar is not always listed on food labels as sugar. Look out for the following terms: sucrose, glucose, fructose, maltose, honey, palm sugar, hydrolysed starch, syrup and invert sugar. Remember, the higher up on the ingredients list, the more of it there is in the product.

HOLISTIC

In a medical sense, 'holistic' refers to the consideration of the whole body. 'Holistic treatment', for example, considers the whole person, including their mind and lifestyle, rather than one symptom in an isolated part of the body.

MSG

A controversial food additive used for flavouring. MSG (monosodium glutamate) is often found in processed foods and fast food. It is generally considered safe, but has been linked to a number of health disorders and negative side effects such as headaches and allergic reactions. Well worth more research if you are going to buy foods containing this liberally added ingredient.

NATURAL, ALL NATURAL, OR 100% NATURAL

A spurious and often misleading term. We align it with healthy or organic food but, on examination, many of the foods which carry this label can be high in sugar, salt, unhealthy fats, and refined ingredients: so-called 'unnatural' ingredients. In fact, the term 'natural' has no regulatory definition in the UK, making it pretty much meaningless.

NUTRIENTS

Macronutrients are the building blocks of our diet: carbohydrates, protein, fibre and fat. Micronutrients are vitamins and minerals (see vitamins and minerals). Foods that provide a good source of both macro- and micronutrients are what I would consider nutrient-dense.

OBESE

An adjective used to describe a person whose body has accumulated so much fat that it is detrimental to their health. A BMI of 30 is generally considered to indicate that a person is obese. Carrying excess weight is a major risk factor for a number of chronic diseases including cancer.

ORGANIC

A term describing food that is produced without the use of chemicals, such as pesticides. Food labelled 'organic' indicates that its system of farming and production has met certain regulatory standards (see also pesticides).

PESCATARIAN

A person who eats fish and seafood, but not meat.

PESTICIDES

Chemicals used in agriculture to destroy insects, fungi, pests, or weeds. This term generally also includes herbicides, fungicide, insect repellent, antimicrobial, avicide, bactericide, insecticides, disinfectant, rodenticide and more. Because of their widespread use, people are exposed to low levels of pesticide residues in their foods. While scientists do not have a clear idea of the health effects of these pesticides, evidence suggests that children are particularly susceptible to adverse effects. We cannot avoid pesticides entirely but buying organic can help us go a long way.

PHYTOCHEMICALS

Compounds found in vegetables that are linked to the possible prevention of chronic disease. Some of the foods they are found in include:

Apples

Apricots

Broccoli

Brussels sprouts

Red peppers

Garlic

Tomatoes

PLANT-BASED

Effectively a vegan diet that comprises only foods derived from plants or the earth. It contains no meat, fish or dairy foods.

POLYPHENOLS

Another class of chemical compound or micronutrient with antioxidant properties found in plants. Polyphenols give plants their colour, and as well as playing a part in the prevention of diabetes, cancer, and neurodegenerative and cardiovascular disease, they can function as a prebiotic. They can be found in foods such as:

Wholefoods

Dried spices

Fruits and vegetables

Red wine

Blueberries

Cacao

PORTION SIZE

How much we should be eating of different foods. For example, we should not be eating more protein than we can hold in the palm of our hands.

POSITIVE EATING

Quite simply, consuming food that is good for us. (Eating well will suffice for me!)

PREBIOTICS

Prebiotics are a type of fibre; not all fibre is prebiotic, but all prebiotics are fibre! They are essentially food for the probiotics (see also probiotics). Prebiotics also work to keep our digestive system happy and protect our immune systems. The more food the probiotics get in the form of prebiotics, the healthier your digestive system is going to be.

Prebiotics exist in many foods, so you are probably ingesting lots of healthy prebiotics and you don't even know it! Since they are a fibre, foods that are high in fibre are often high in prebiotics. Some foods high in prebiotics include:

Garlic

Onion

Leeks

Asparagus

Bananas

Oats

Barley

Apples

Cocoa (it its pure form, not mixed with all the milk and sugar that turns this into a junk food)

Flax seeds

Chicory root

Wheatbran

Seaweed

Artichokes

PROBIOTICS

Live, beneficial bacteria, or microorganisms and yeasts that are good for your digestive system and therefore you! Probiotics live inside the gastrointestinal tract and keep everything flowing by affecting nerves that control gut movements. As such, they can help treat IBS (inflammatory bowel syndrome) and other bowel disorders.

Probiotics can be found in yoghurts and other fermented foods, such as kefir and kombucha, but you can also consider taking a course of probiotic supplements every few months to boost your system. As with all supplements, check that the brand is reputable. It should have a minimum of 10 billion live organisms per dosage. It is also worth noting that not all capsules are vegetarian. Some are also appropriate for children.

PROTEIN

An essential macronutrient for the body and one of the building blocks for tissue such as bones, muscles, and cartilage, as well as a source of fuel. Proteins are large complex molecules that comprise 20 different types of amino acids. We also need it to repair our bodies and to make enzymes, hormones, and other vital body chemicals.

RECOMMENDED INTAKE (RI)

Formerly known as recommended daily allowance (RDA), RI refers to the maximum amount of nutrients of calories that you should consume each day.

REFINED FOODS

Foods that have been processed: in other words, altered during their preparation. As a general rule, the more refined your foods are, the less goodness they have left in them. The body has to do less work to digest refined foods and carbohydrates are turned into sugar more quickly. As a result, you get a spike of energy after eating refined foods, but this is followed by a crash.

SALT

A mineral that comes in various forms. Table salt is harvested from deposits found underground. It is highly refined, contains impurities and trace minerals, and is often treated with anticaking agents. Table salt may also contain iodine. I would advise you never to use this.

Sea salt is produced through the evaporation of seawater, while rock salt, sometimes known as halite, is a mineral formed from sodium chloride. It is found in the rock beds of dried up lakes and seas and contains a number of trace elements. Both are usually made with minimal processing and no additives, however it is always worth checking labels.

Himalayan salt is arguably the purest form of salt in the world. Off-white to pink in colour, it originates from the Himalayan mountains in Pakistan and it is said to contain the 84 natural minerals and elements found in the human body. If your budget allows, I would recommend using Himalayan salt.

SODIUM

The scientific term for salt.

SUGAR

A sweet-tasting carbohydrate. Some sugars are better for the body than others, though my general advice would be to minimise your intake of sugar as much as possible, as it is a leading cause of obesity and chronic disease, and the body simply doesn't need it. Many foods that you might not expect contain sugar (see hidden sugars). If you must use them, look for unrefined sugars, ideally organic. The only sweeteners I have in the house are:

Organic coconut sugar

Organic unrefined jaggery

Organic coconut nectar

Organic manuka honey (unique manuka factor (UMF) value above 10)

Organic dates or date nectar

These sweeteners don't have the same negative spike of energy associated with refined sugars and have some nutrient value. Manuka honey, for example, has anti-inflammatory and antibacterial properties. It also protects immunity and supports recovery from colds and flu.

SUGAR-FREE

A product that would usually contain sugar, but has had it removed. Usually, the sugar is replaced by something that isn't necessarily doing you any good, and in some cases may be worse. Approach with caution and scrutinise the labels.

SUPERFOOD

A term used to describe foods that are thought to deliver exceptional levels of nutrition in respect of antioxidants, energy, vitamin and mineral profile, or other identified health benefits.

First used in the early 21st century, the term 'superfood' has become more and more spurious. A lot of so-called 'superfoods' originally came from outside the UK, such as chia seeds (which have stood the test of time), baobab, maca, spirulina, chlorella and lucuma. Since then, a whole industry has developed around the concept, with people hoping to meet all their nutritional needs with a few exceptional foods.

The reality is that these foods really can boast a fantastic nutritional profile. Maca, for example, is an adaptogen-like ginseng, so it works in sync with our body to balance what needs balancing and support our system. However, the more I learn about food, the more I see that the everyday foods we are very used to – almost exclusively in the plant-based world – are full of 'super powers' too. If you are choosing and consuming the right foods, there is no need to spend lots of money on exotic ingredients.

VEGAN

A person who eats only plant-based foods and nothing animal-based, such as dairy or meat. The word vegan usually translates to a whole way of life or philosophy around animal products and values.

VEGETARIAN

A person who eats no meat or fish, but will eat animal products, such as eggs and cheese.

VITAMINS AND MINERALS

Essential micronutrients for the body. For optimal health, the body needs 13 essential vitamins: A, B (which includes 8 vitamins), C, D, E and K, each of which performs a very specific role. We also require a range of vital minerals. While all vitamins are needed by the body, only some minerals are needed for good health.

Vitamins are made by living things, and we get them through eating plants and animal-based products. They are fairly complex organic substances, but can be destroyed by high heat and cooking. Most of us will get all the vitamins we need from a balanced diet, but some may benefit from a supplement.

Minerals, on the other hand, are found in the earth and as such are simple inorganic substances. They are robust in that they cannot be broken down by sunlight or heat. Examples of minerals that we need include: calcium, magnesium, iron, zinc and potassium. They can be found in a number of foods, from meat and fish to vegetables, dried fruit and nuts.

WHOLEGRAIN

Grain that has not been refined to retain only the endosperm, as a lot of over-processed white breads and foods have. A wholegrain diet is associated with good health and a lower risk of many diseases. Examples of wholegrains include:

Barley

Rye

Bulgar wheat (cracked wheat)

Oatmeal

Wholewheat products

Buckwheat

Popcorn (naked, without the unhealthy additions)

Quinoa

Brown rice

Spelt and spelt-derived products.

YEAST

A fungus. There are many different types, but brewer's yeast (used to make beer) is probably the most common. Yeast is also used to make bread. While it can boast a range of B vitamins, yeast is frequently added as a flavouring to many savoury foods, which can lead to an overgrowth in our system, called candida, which can be detrimental to health. Check all labels and avoid foods with yeast as an additive (see also antifungal).

CAREY DAVIS-MUNRO

Carey Davis-Munro has over 25 years' experience in the field of health, fitness and wellbeing. Her previous roles include Physical Education teacher, Learning and Development and HR Professional (CIPD qualified), serial entrepreneur and creator of the UK's first to market multi-award-winning Superfood Healthy Chocolate Truffles.

Carey works as a Food and Wellbeing Coach with businesses and individuals, empowering people to build a healthier relationship with food for long-term wellness as well as physical and mental agility. Having run food workshops for years, Carey is also a motivational speaker on the subject of nutrition, telling her own story and examining the psychology behind healthy eating and how to bring a family along with you on the journey to optimum health. Her key message is about urging people to prioritise their health, and to do so through the single biggest influence on lifestyle diseases: food.

Carey is already a published author, having had many of her recipes reproduced by Ocado on the health-focused section of the online supermarket's website. She is also a regular radio and podcast presenter on Wellbeing Radio and other platforms.

Carey lives in Middlesex and is a mum to three teenagers. She realised that her priorities needed to change when diagnosed with stress-induced chronic fatigue, brought on by her body 'crashing' while she refused to listen to the signs. Carey needed to become well enough not only to have children, but to be around for a very long time in order to be part of their lives and support them. Food was the answer. Passionate about the power and potential it holds as the fulcrum for good health, Carey now guides others to make their relationship with food central to their own lives.